UNMASKING
JEZEBEL'S
INTERCESSORS

Destiny Image Books by Jennifer LeClaire

Deliverance from Prophetic Witchcraft

Exposing Prophetic Witchcraft

Cleansing Your Home from Evil

The Making of a Watchman

Decoding the Mysteries of Heaven's War Room

Discerning Prophetic Witchcraft

Your End Times Prayer Secret

Victory Decrees

The Seer Dimensions

The Spiritual Warrior's Guide to Defeating Water Spirits

The Prophet's Devotional

Tongues of Fire

UNMASKING
JEZEBEL'S
INTERCESSORS

CONQUER THE DEMONIC SPIRIT
HIJACKING WHAT GOD IS BUILDING IN YOUR LIFE

JENNIFER LeCLAIRE

© Copyright 2024– Jennifer LeClaire

All rights reserved. This book is protected by the copyright laws of the United States of America. This book may not be copied or reprinted for commercial gain or profit. The use of short quotations or occasional page copying for personal or group study is permitted and encouraged. Permission will be granted upon request. Scripture quotations marked NKJV are taken from the New King James Version. Copyright © 1982 by Thomas Nelson, Inc. Used by permission. All rights reserved. Scripture quotations marked AMPC are taken from the Amplified® Bible, Classic Edition, Copyright © 1954, 1958, 1962, 1964, 1965, 1987 by The Lockman Foundation. All rights reserved. Used by permission. Scripture quotations marked ESV are taken from The Holy Bible, English Standard Version® (ESV®), copyright © 2001 by Crossway, a publishing ministry of Good News Publishers. Used by permission. All rights reserved. Scripture quotations marked KJV are taken from the King James Version. Scripture quotations marked NASB are taken from the NEW AMERICAN STANDARD BIBLE®, Copyright © 1960, 1962, 1963, 1968, 1971, 1972, 1973, 1975, 1977, 1995, 2020 by The Lockman Foundation. Used by permission. Scripture quotations marked TPT are taken from The Passion Translation, Copyright © 2017, 2018, 2020 by Passion & Fire Ministries, Inc., www.thepassiontranslation.com. Used by permission of BroadStreet Publishing Group, LLC, Racine, Wisconsin, USA. All rights reserved. Scripture quotations marked NIV are taken from the HOLY BIBLE, NEW INTERNATIONAL VERSION®, Copyright © 1973, 1978, 1984, 2011 International Bible Society. Used by permission of Zondervan. All rights reserved. Scripture quotations marked MSG are taken from *The Message*. Copyright © 1993, 1994, 1995, 1996, 2000, 2001, 2002. Used by permission of NavPress Publishing Group. Used by permission. All rights reserved. Scripture quotations marked NLT are taken from the Holy Bible, New Living Translation, copyright 1996, 2004, 2015. Used by permission of Tyndale House Publishers., Wheaton, Illinois 60189. All rights reserved. Scripture quotations marked CEV are taken from the Contemporary English Version Copyright © 1995 by the American Bible Society, New York, NY. All rights reserved. Scripture quotations marked MEV are taken from *The Holy Bible, Modern English Version*. Copyright © 2014 by Military Bible Association. Published and distributed by Charisma House. All rights reserved. Used by permission. Scripture quotations marked CSB are taken from the Christian Standard Bible. Copyright © 2017 by Holman Bible Publishers. Used by permission. Christian Standard Bible®, and CSB® are federally registered trademarks of Holman Bible Publishers, all rights reserved. Scripture quotations marked DRA are taken from the Douay-Rheims 1899 American Edition. Public domain. Take note that the name satan and related names are not capitalized. We choose not to acknowledge him, even to the point of violating grammatical rules.

DESTINY IMAGE® PUBLISHERS, INC.
P.O. Box 310, Shippensburg, PA 17257-0310
"Publishing cutting-edge prophetic resources to supernaturally empower the body of Christ"

This book and all other Destiny Image and Destiny Image Fiction books are available at Christian bookstores and distributors worldwide.

For more information on foreign distributors, call 717-532-3040.

Reach us on the Internet: www.destinyimage.com.

ISBN 13 TP: 978-0-7684-6438-2

ISBN 13 eBook: 978-0-7684-6439-9

For Worldwide Distribution, Printed in the U.S.A.

1 2 3 4 5 6 7 8 / 28 27 26 25 24

DEDICATION

I dedicate this book to my Awakening Prayer Hubs leaders who have stayed the course through thick and thin—and through every Jezebelic assignment against us. It's my honor to lead a prayer army in the nations that is making an impact now and in eternity. More Holy Ghost power to you.

CONTENTS

Introduction 11

Chapter 1   Hello, My Name Is Jezebel. 15

Chapter 2   Intercessors of Light. 31

Chapter 3   Intercessors of Darkness 45

Chapter 4   Why Jezebel Is Attracted to Intercession 61

Chapter 5   Why Jezebel's Intercessors Are so Dangerous 81

Chapter 6   Protection, Power, and Prestige. 97

Chapter 7   Prophesying, Teaching, Undermining, and Dominating . . 115

Chapter 8   Grooming Sons, Spies, Messengers, and False Prophets 131

Chapter 9   Avoiding Tapping into Witchcraft Prayers 145

Chapter 10 Confronting Jezebel's Intercessors 161

Chapter 11 Dealing with Jezebel's Aftermath 179

Chapter 12 What Jezebel's Intercessors Don't Want You to Know . . . 191

About Jennifer LeClaire. 205

INTRODUCTION

At Christian International's 50th International Gathering of Apostles and Prophets in 2017, Bishop Bill Hamon ordained me as a prophet with an audience of thousands of people around the world. Given he is the father of the modern-day prophetic movement and has pioneered prophetic ministries in the nations, this was one of the greatest honors of my life.

Although I had previously been ordained and had been walking in the office of the prophet for many years, the public ceremony was a demonstration of the formal alignment and commitment to my spiritual father and the pure prophetic movement.

At the end of the service, an usher was escorting me into a back room when Bishop suddenly grabbed my arm and redirected my steps. Surely, it was the Holy Spirit leading him to lead me because suddenly I ran into Chuck Pierce, founder of Glory of Zion. Chuck was about to leave, but as divine timing would have it we crossed paths.

When Chuck saw me he stopped and said, "I'm glad I ran into you. I have something for you." I was shocked. I had no idea what he was going to do or say. He pulled out a mantle, wrapped it around me, and proceeded to prophesy that God had called me to raise up prophets to throw Jezebel off the wall. With the new commissioning came a new assignment—and new warfare with the spirit of Jezebel.

Since Chuck released that pivotal prophetic word, I have diligently endeavored to fulfill the divine mandate. I have been to many nations on several continents to expose Jezebel's work in the prophetic movement. What I quickly learned was this: Where you find Jezebel's prophets, you'll find Jezebel's intercessors. That's because while not all intercessors are not prophets, all prophets are intercessors.

I wrote this book, *Unmasking Jezebel's Intercessors*, as part of the prophesied assignment to *accurately* expose Jezebel in the nations. I say "accurately expose" because if you haven't already noticed, there's plenty of disinformation circulating about Jezebel. Indeed, if you type "spirit of Jezebel" into Google you will get 5.2 million results in less than a quarter of a second. It's a testament to the pervasiveness of this spirit and a show of how many people have differing opinions on what this spirit is and how it operates.

Please, hear me: Much of what you read about the spirit of Jezebel is either completely wrong, only partly right, or mostly hype. Much of what you read will not help you overcome Jezebel but will send you on a witch hunt—or cause you to engage in a spiritual battle with what you think is Jezebel while the real Jezebel has her way. This leads to spiritual and natural frustration and more damage.

While sharing personal experiences can be helpful to illustrate a point, experience without scriptural backing is often less than accurate and at times even skewed by personal biases. Yes, we will have experiences with Jezebel's intercessors that don't match up with chapter and verse in Scripture. But many are coming up with outlandish conclusions about the characteristics of Jezebel that lead people astray while Jezebel continues to entrench herself in lives, families, workplaces, cities, and nations. Again, the real Jezebel stays hidden in our ignorance.

While we can find the fruit of a Jezebel spirit operating through people in Scripture, we must be careful not to use a single experience to cement truth and create stereotypes that could be steeped in presumption—presumption that could sully the truth that would otherwise set us free from Jezebelic attacks. Put another way, we don't want to create our own theology about Jezebel's intercessors and teach based on that experience alone. That's how false Jezebel accusations start flying while the real Jezebel gets further entrenched in your prayer group. (Read that again slowly.)

We don't want to cast Jezebelic aspersions on people based on our own personal run-ins with this spirit alone. We want the Holy Spirit's discernment to identify Jezebel's intercessors and His wisdom to get them healed and delivered—or to root them out of our midst. We don't want to tick the boxes, so to speak, of the signs and symptoms devoid of the Holy Spirit's leading.

I wrote this book to blow the lid off Jezebel's intercessors, which too few see until it's too late. I share my experiences from decades of dealing with these demons in prayer meetings so you can see clear examples of how this spirit works in the context of intercession. But this book, like all my books, is heavy on Scripture because we need to stay rooted in the Word of God.

Through the pages of this book, you will surely have "aha" moments as the Holy Spirit connects the dots and you see the full picture of past and present Jezebelic intercessors in your midst. My hope and prayer is that this book brings confirmation, revelation, and wisdom on how to deal with the present and future Jezebels that will surely infiltrate your prayer meeting sooner or later.

CHAPTER 1

HELLO, MY NAME IS JEZEBEL

Mick Jagger of *Rolling Stones* fame took a lot of heat for writing a song called "Sympathy for the Devil" in 1968. The song starts out with these lyrics, which were written from satan's perspective: "Please allow me to introduce myself, I'm a man of wealth and taste. I've been around for long, long years, stole million man's soul and faith. ...Pleased to meet you, hope you guess my name."

Satan doesn't typically walk into your business or church and introduce himself—and neither does Jezebel. Demon powers work hard to fly under your radar screen so they can do damage before you discern them. Jezebels slip in to prayer meetings, church congregations, business, schools—and anywhere else they can—without God's leadership or approval. And Jezebel never walks in with a name badge that says, "Hello, my name is Jezebel." She never walks in and announces, "I'm here to steal your intercessors, kill the anointing, and destroy your prayer ministry. I'm here to woo your employees to myself, derail your reputation, and turn people against you."

No, I've never once seen Jezebel introduce herself as a false intercessor who is intent on wreaking havoc on God's plans and purposes through witchcraft prayers and a cadre of other satanic strategies and tactics. Jezebel, rather, usually walks into your life with a bright smile, a diehard commitment to intercession, and often an eloquence that mimics a powerful prayer anointing. Indeed, Jezebel's intercessors can be difficult to immediately discern.

No, Jezebel never walks into your midst manifesting the characteristics of the prophet-killing demon we all know and hate—and want to avoid. No, she doesn't tip her hand until after she secures her place in your inner circle. She comes across as faithful and unassuming, with what appears to be a servant's heart. She is willing to do anything and everything she can to forward God's will in your midst. Make no mistake. It's a ploy and if you fall for it, you'll pay a hefty price.

Because Jezebel's intercessors can be so difficult to discern, leaders of companies, churches, clubs, or prayer ministries are often shocked when they discover Jezebel has been moving undercover in their midst for months or even years. The awful revelation and grim reality that Jezebel has a toehold, a foothold, or even a stronghold in your organization is beyond dreadful.

Because Jezebel's intercessors have done such great damage to both secular and Christian organizations, an unfortunate phenomenon has arisen. Many assertive, New York-attitude, type-A personalities have walked in prayer meetings with a passionate heart to see God's Kingdom come and His will be done on earth as it is in heaven only to be immediately marked as Jezebels and shunned.

Too many have been painted with what amounts to a "scarlet letter" by jealous intercessors who are intimidated by a true anointing.

Here's my point: We do not want to let Jezebel in disguise derail our prayer efforts. But we don't want to make false accusations against sincere or immature intercessors either. (We'll talk more about these unfortunate witch hunts later.) To avoid both these scenarios, wisdom dictates understanding what the Jezebel spirit really is and what it is not. Make no mistake, Jezebel will drop by your company, church, club, or prayer group to say hello at some point if she hasn't already. And she will try to drive out the true intercessors.

JEZEBEL: A CASE OF MISTAKEN IDENTITY

When it comes to Jezebel, we can't afford cases of mistaken identity—labeling people Jezebel who are not while the real Jezebel wreaks havoc incognito. But it happens all the time because there are so many erroneous teachings about the essence of Jezebel.

Contrary to the secular proverb, something can walk like a duck and quack like a duck and not be a duck. Let me put it another way: Have you ever heard the notion that everyone has a twin in the world somewhere? This notion asserts there's someone out there who looks almost just like you but is not you. (Or if you are an actual twin, you may literally know someone who looks exactly like you.) In either scenario, that lookalike is not you. That walking, quacking duck is not you. Nevertheless, you could easily face a case of mistaken identity.

Such was the case with two African-American men in the early 1900s.[1] A man named Will West was convicted of a crime and put in prison at Leavenworth. The prison clerk took a mug shot, wrote down a physical description, and took measurements of the inmate. Based on the photos and measurements, investigators matched him to another man with a similar name: William West.

William West had been convicted of murder. Will West denied knowing the murderous man. But their photos were nearly identical. When shown the photo, Will West said, "That's my picture, but I don't know where you got it, for I know I have never been here before." It turned out William West was already jailed in the same prison serving a life sentence. Only fingerprints could tell them apart. And that is why, when people are arrested today, officers take fingerprints.

It's no different with Jezebel. Many people mistake other spirits for Jezebel and mistake Jezebel with other spirits. Various spirits can look a lot alike because all demons seek to steal, kill, and destroy (see John 10:10). We need to fingerprint the spirits, so to speak, to rightly identify the culprit. Or should I say, we need the Holy Spirit to provide us with fingerprints in the manner of spiritual discernment.

After decades of battle, this principality called Jezebel remains one of the most popular principalities on the spiritual warfare scene. But often we have a case of mistaken identity, and many are wounded by being falsely labeled as a "Jezebel." Ironically, that wound can open the door to the Jezebel spirit, since Jezebel often targets the hurt and wounded. It is indeed a potentially vicious cycle. And Jezebel loves it.

JEZEBEL HIDES BEHIND A MAN-MADE MASK

Jezebel hides behind the mask of manipulation and control, but let's be clear: Jezebel is not a spirit of manipulation and control.

Because so many books with differing theologies around Jezebel have been penned over the last number of decades, there are myths and misconceptions about the Jezebel spirit that dilute true Holy Spirit discernment. We tend to look too much at flesh and blood personality traits, like a take-charge attitude, or Internet checklists to diagnose a Jezebel in our midst.

Again, many tend to think Jezebel is a spirit of control, manipulation, or domination when in fact control, manipulation, and domination are simply a means to an end for Jezebel. Jezebel hides behind these behaviors so you can't see the ultimate motive, which is seduction. Many have worked from an incomplete revelation of who Jezebel is and therefore cannot discern or defeat this spirit. In that way, they tolerate Jezebel, which is dangerous.

If you think the Jezebel spirit is just a spirit of control or manipulation—or even the hunger for power—you're going to miss the real Jezebel. If you miss the real Jezebel, you'll end up falling for the strategies of this wicked personality who is influencing the minds of people—and even turning them against you without your knowledge. By throwing some false flags, the real Jezebel can distract you and catch you off guard while she sneaks around in your midst sowing seeds of discord.

I've been part of churches where people are labeled Jezebels shortly after they walk in the door. They are marked as controllers and manipulators who want to get close to the pastor for power and position. The reality is they may be controllers and manipulators, or they may not be. The real controllers and manipulators are more often, in my experience, the ones slinging the misguided Jezebel accusations.

As I write in my book *The Spiritual Warrior's Guide to Defeating Jezebel,* Jezebel is not a woman with a strong personality who just needs some people skills. Jezebel is not a woman who needs to read *How to Win Friends and Influence People.* And by the way, Jezebel can operate through a man or a woman. Jezebel is an androgynous spirit, having the characteristics of both men and women. We sometimes refer to this spirit as "she" because it manifested in women in the pages of the Bible.

An abusive church leader once insisted he saw a Jezebel spirit superimposed over my body and that I was in danger of giving myself over to Jezebel if I didn't step in line with his wishes. I was certainly alarmed, so I submitted myself to several pastors outside that church for a thorough examination. One of the pastors asked me a startling question:

"Are you seducing people?"

"No!" I exclaimed, not understanding why he would ask such a thing.

"Are you leading people away from Jesus?"

"Of course, not!" I said.

"Then you aren't operating in a Jezebel spirit."

That set me free and helped me see where the true Jezebel was operating.

Along with "false prophet," a Jezebel accusation is one of the most serious fiery darts you can throw at a believer. It implies that they aren't a believer at all but that they are fornicators who will not inherit the Kingdom of God and false brethren who are purposefully leading people away from Christ for their own gain.

WILL THE REAL JEZEBEL PLEASE STAND UP?

In the 1950s and 1960s there was a game show called *To Tell the Truth* that intrigued the masses. In the show we find a panel of four celebrities who are charged with identifying who is telling the truth about their identity. The host reads a bio about the character's unusual occupation or experience and then three challengers try to convince the celebrities they are the character in question.

Two of the challengers are imposters. Only one of the three is the real character. The two challengers make up false answers to the questions the celebrities ask. Only the true character tells the truth about who they are. At the end of the show, the host asks, "Will the real So and So please stand up?" The celebrities and the audience are often shocked at how convincing the liars were. We need to see the real Jezebel. (Check out my course, "Will the Real Jezebel Please Stand Up?" at www.schoolofthespirit.tv.)

So who is Jezebel and where did this terminology come from? Many say there is no such thing as a Jezebel spirit, but once you've seen the patterns of how this spirit operates you can't deny its reality. Jezebel was the name of a pagan queen who married King Ahab in Scripture. She served the false gods Ashtoreth and Baal.

Ultimately, we're not dealing with Jezebel. We're dealing with the goddess Ashtoreth that Jezebel served. We're dealing with the spirit that morphed the wicked queen's personality. That's because we become like the one we behold. Consider Paul's Spirit-inspired words in 2 Corinthians 3:18 (NKJV), "But we all, with unveiled face, beholding as in a mirror the glory of the Lord, are being transformed into the same image from glory to glory, just as by the Spirit of the Lord." The wicked queen Jezebel was beholding Ashtoreth.

Ashtoreth is the Queen of Heaven, the female counterpart to Baal. She is known as the wife of Baal and was the high goddess of Canaan. Indeed, she is the goddess of love and war. According to the *International Standard Bible Encyclopedia*, prostitution was practiced in the name of Ashtoreth and prophetesses were attached to her temples to whom she delivered oracles.

Ashtoreth is the very goddess that Israel worshipped during its times of apostasy (see Judges 2:13; 1 Sam. 7:3-4; 2 Kings 23:13). Ashtoreth is the goddess of love and war. Ashtoreth is the chief god that Old Testament Jezebel served. In fact, Jezebel's father, Ethbaal, was the high priest of the goddess Ashtoreth. Some believers are unwittingly serving Ashtoreth today.

Ashtoreth was Jezebel's key influence. And we see the damage Queen Jezebel did in Israel. Jezebel seduced Ahab and many in Israel into idolatry, which essentially led them into bondage and God's judgment of famine for three and a half years. Jezebel massacred the true prophets of the Lord while keeping the false prophets on her payroll, eating plenty from her table in a time of famine (see 1 Kings 18:13-19). Jezebel had Naboth killed and stole his inheritance.

JEZEBEL THE SEDUCTRESS

Note that Jezebel did all this, ultimately, through the power of seduction. Indeed, Jezebel is, at its essence, a spirit of seduction. We could just as easily say we're battling the spirit of seduction. We call this demon Jezebel because both the Queen Jezebel and the woman Jezebel from Thyatira in the Book of Revelation carried this name and demonstrated the same demonic traits. One was thrown down and devoured by dogs. The other was threatened with a sick bed. Both were judgments on Jezebel.

Jesus identifies the root of what we call the spirit of Jezebel, a common term we can all use to identity the spirit (just like doctors use the term *cancer* in all nations to identify the deadly disease that destroys normal body tissue), and He gives one of the sternest warnings in Scripture. Revelation 2:18-29 (NKJV) reads:

> *And to the angel of the church in Thyatira write, "These things says the Son of God, who has eyes like a flame of fire, and His feet like fine brass: 'I know your works, love, service, faith, and your patience; and as for your works, the last are more than the first. Nevertheless I have a few things against you, because you allow that woman Jezebel, who calls herself a prophetess, to teach and seduce My servants to commit sexual immorality and eat things sacrificed to idols. And I gave her time to repent of her sexual immorality, and she did not repent. Indeed I will cast her into a sickbed, and those who commit adultery with her into great tribulation, unless they repent of their deeds. I will kill her children with death, and all the churches shall know that I am He who searches the minds and hearts. And I will give to each one of you according to your works.*
>
> *"'Now to you I say, and to the rest in Thyatira, as many as do not have this doctrine, who have not known the depths of Satan, as they say, I will put on you no other burden. But hold fast what you have till I come. And he who overcomes, and keeps My works until the end,*

> to him I will give power over the nations—"He shall rule them with a rod of iron; they shall be dashed to pieces like the potter's vessels"—as I also have received from My Father; and I will give him the morning star. He who has an ear, let him hear what the Spirit says to the churches.'"

Notice the command not to tolerate Jezebel. People often tolerate it because they don't discern it, or because there's no one else to help with the tasks at hand—or because they are big donors. There are many reasons why people tolerate intercessors operating in a Jezebel spirit. All of them lead to destruction.

Easton's Bible Dictionary says this of Queen Jezebel, "Jezebel has stamped her name on history as the representative of all that is designing, crafty, malicious, revengeful, and cruel. She is the first great instigator of persecution against the saints of God. Guided by no principle, restrained by no fear of either God or man, passionate in her attachment to her heathen worship, she spared no pains to maintain idolatry around her in all its splendour."[2] And *Matthew Henry's Commentary* calls Jezebel a "zealous idolater, extremely imperious and malicious in her natural temper, addicted to witchcrafts and whoredoms, and every way vicious."[3]

AN END-TIMES ASSIGNMENT

I believe we are in the end times. I believe God is raising up prayer and worship movements around the world to prepare for the Second Coming of Christ. And I believe that is why we're seeing Jezebel manifest with greater bravado now than in decades past. Indeed, the late Lester Sumrall once said Jezebel would be one of the greatest opponents in the end-times church. Perhaps that's why there's so much emphasis on Jezebel in the Book of Revelation.

Keep in mind, intercessors are among those who are uniquely positioned to throw Jezebel down through spiritual warfare prayer. But you can't throw Jezebel off the wall if you don't dwell on the wall. Intercessors who live on the wall of intercession—those who watch and pray day and night, night and day—gain a position of authority to throw Jezebel down.

You can't dwell on the wall until you build the wall. In this season, God is looking for intercessors who will make a wall, stand on it, and actually dwell on it to prevent Jezebel from gaining further inroads of destruction in families, churches, and cities.

God is emphasizing Ezekiel 22:30 (NKJV) in this hour: "So I sought for a man among them who would make a wall, and stand in the gap before Me on behalf of the land, that I should not destroy it; but I found no one."

When Joshua sent two spies into Jericho, the spies entered Rahab's house. When the king found out about it, he sent men to her house to take the Israelites captive. Instead of handing them over, she made a wall of intercession. Rahab told the king's men the Hebrews had escaped—then helped them escape. Consider this act of intercession in Joshua 2, understanding that one definition of intercession is "interpose." *Interpose* means to intervene or to put a barrier or obstacle between or in the way of, according to Dictionary.com.

> *Then Rahab lowered them by a rope through the window, for her home was set into the wall where she lived. She said to them, "Go to the hill country so that the pursuers do not find you. Hide there three days until the pursuers return. After that, you can go on your way"* (Joshua 2:15-16 MEV).

Since her house was on the wall, she could provide a way of escape even when the gate was shut. Her intercession was their only hope of deliverance from the enemy. Rahab offered an act of intercession that saved the lives of two Israelites on a mission from God. But God rewarded her intercession by saving her entire family.

Intercessors who live on the wall have a perspective that can only be attained by living on the wall. Some intercessors only see the wall the enemy has erected. Other intercessors try to peek over the wall to see what God is doing. Intercessors who live on the wall can see further out into the spirit, gain God's view into the situation, and tap into a divine prayer strategy to see His will come to pass.

Rahab lived on the wall. No doubt, she prayed on the wall. And when the walls of Jericho came crashing down, God's wall of protection preserved Rahab and her family. Her act of intercession paved the way for God's will and also paved the way for the Messiah, who was birthed through her family line (see Matt. 4:1-6). Only intercessors who build the wall and then live on the wall are positioned to throw Jezebel off the wall. These are Nehemiah intercessors who build with one hand and carry a weapon in the other hand (see Neh. 4:17).

Intercessors who build walls of prayer have a distinct authority to throw down spirits that try to penetrate that wall or erect a stronghold on that wall. Intercessors who live on the wall incline their ear to the Lord's command to throw Jezebel down at the right moment.

The right moment is now. We're in a Jehu moment—a Jehu season to throw Jezebel down. In 2 Kings 9:32-34 (NKJV) Jehu:

> *Looked up at the window, and said, "Who is on my side? Who?" So two or three eunuchs looked out at him. Then he said, "Throw her down." So they threw her down, and some of her blood spattered on the wall and on the horses; and he trampled her underfoot. And when he had gone in, he ate and drank. Then he said, "Go now, see to this accursed woman, and bury her, for she was a king's daughter."*

It's time to throw Jezebel down in your family, your church, and your workplace. Again, you do this in the place of prayer. And after you throw her down, bury all memory of her. Move on with your life in victory!

ANTICIPATING JEZEBEL'S ENTRANCE

This bears repeating. Whether you have a prayer group or Bible study or lead a team in the workplace, if you are in a place of prayer Jezebel's intercessors will drop by to say hello. If you don't discern it and shut it down quickly in the spirit, you will have more than a handful of problems to deal with. Jezebel will usurp your authority and defile the purity of other intercessors.

My purpose for writing this book is not so you can go on a witch hunt and make false accusations like in the Salem Witch Trials that saw innocent people killed. Consider the words of C.S. Lewis in *The Screwtape Letters*, "There are two equal and opposite errors into which our race can fall about the devils. One is to disbelieve in their existence. The other is to believe, and to feel an excessive and unhealthy interest in them. They themselves are equally pleased by both errors and hail a materialist or a magician with the same delight."[4]

My purpose is to equip you to discern Jezebel's intercessors so you can throw that spirit down and out of your midst. Again, don't go on a witch hunt that grieves the Lord and harms true intercessors who are under spiritual attack, immature, or hurt and wounded. Discern and deal with the spirit. Love the people.

Always remember, Jezebel can influence anyone. I'm reminded of a poet named W.H. Auden. In 1942, he asked a group of Sunday school students what seemed to be a strange question: "Do you know what the devil looks like?" His answer was plain and thought provoking: "The devil looks like me." We need to examine our hearts to be sure there is no wicked way in us. We need to pull the log out of our eye before we deal with the beam in someone else's eye.

MY PRAYER FOR YOU

I pray, in the name of Jesus, as you read this book you will grow in a revelation of Jezebel's operations and in the confidence and authority to shut down every insidious infiltration of this wicked spirit. I pray that you will take your authority swiftly over Jezebel's witchcraft in the name of Jesus. Amen.

NOTES

1. Rare Historical Photos, "The Will and William West case: The identical inmates that showed the need for fingerprinting, 1903," November 28, 2021, https://rarehistoricalphotos.com/will-william-west-case-fingerprints.

2. M.G. Easton, *Easton's Bible Dictionary,* s.v. "Jezebel," (Thomas Nelson, 1897), https://biblehub.com/topical/j/jezebel.htm.

3. Matthew Henry, *Matthew Henry's Commentary,* s.v. 1 Kings 16, (1706), https://www.blueletterbible.org/Comm/mhc/1Ki/1Ki_016.cfm.

4. C.S. Lewis, *The Screwtape Letters* (London: Centenary Press, 1942), preface.

CHAPTER 2

INTERCESSORS OF LIGHT

The first known lighthouse dates to 280 B.C. Known as Pharos of Alexandria in Egypt, it stood at more than 350 feet high and was one of the seven wonders of the ancient world. Pharos of Alexandria is no longer standing, but many historic lighthouses still are.

While most of them are mere landmarks—they no longer serve any practical purpose—those lighthouses played a critical role in the success of captains navigating dangerous seas. Lighthouses, for example, served to warn sailors of dangerous shallows and perilous rocky coasts that could leave them shipwrecked. Lighthouses likewise helped lead and guide mariners to safe harbor. Put another way, lighthouses say, "Beware of danger" or "Come to safety." Indeed, lighthouses saved lives.

In centuries past, every lighthouse had a lightkeeper. A lightkeeper was charged with making sure the light and the lens were maintained and that fuel was replenished so the lighthouse could function rightly. The lightkeeper might be compared to a keeper of the flame in Leviticus 6:9 (NKJV), "The burnt offering shall be on the hearth upon the altar all night until morning, and the fire of the altar shall be kept burning on it."

Intercessors are modern-day keepers of the flame. The fire of intercession must never cease. We must pray without ceasing. Our light, of course, is the Word. The Word of God is a lamp unto our feet and a light unto our path (see Ps. 119:105). The Word of God is like fire (see Jer. 5:14). While Jezebel's intercessors operate in darkness, Jesus' intercessors operate in the light and work to expose the darkness that keeps souls in bondage, cities in disarray, and nations captive. Jezebel calls intercessors into darkness. Jesus calls intercessors of light.

GOD IS CALLING FORTH INTERCESSORS OF LIGHT

I had never heard anyone speak of "intercessors of light." The Holy Spirit Himself was the first person I heard say these words. With that, I prophesied at length about intercessors of light. See, there are intercessors of light and intercessors of darkness. There are Holy Spirit-inspired intercessors and demon-inspired intercessors. We need to learn the difference. I believe if you are reading this book, you are an intercessor of light—or God wants to make you one.

I heard the Lord say: "I am calling forth intercessors of light whom I can trust to send into the dark places, into places where demonic strongholds have been a reality for the people living in foreign lands for centuries. I am calling forth intercessors of light and intercessors of life who will pray without ceasing with words of life in their mouth—prayers of life emanating by the Holy Spirit, spoken forth by your mouths.

"Yield your light to Me, and yield your life to Me, and yield your mouth to Me, for I am sending you on assignment to dark places to let your light shine, and your light will overcome the darkness. Your light will shine in the darkness. The darkness will not overcome your light. I am sending you on intercessory assignments to do My bidding, even in the darkest places. You may not step foot on the land, but your prayers will invade the land and souls will be saved because a light will come on and they will see Me and they will know Me.

"And the Gospel will reach their heart—the Gospel will reach their heart, and the Gospel will reach their soul, and they will say yes to Me because of your prayers. So do not be afraid of the darkness and do not be afraid of the retaliation. Do not be afraid of the wicked one because the winning One is in you. I am always going to win every battle in which I engage, so when I send you as an intercessor of light, you will win. You will execute My will. You will see the blessings for engaging in the battle. You will gather the spoils of war. You will see eternal rewards.

"Get in My Word! For the entrance of My Word brings light. For yes, you will be resisted in your assignment, but My light will keep you from the darkness, from the powers of wickedness, from the effects of the demon powers who are lobbing bombs at you, lobbing grenades at you, firing darts at you. Your faith will stay strong as you let the entrance of My Word bring light into your soul.

"Your faith will rise because faith comes by hearing and hearing by the Word, and your faith will cause you to outlast the enemy of your soul who is trying to get you to give up. For intercessors of light do not quit, they do not faint, and they do not falter because My life is in them. So yield to My light."

CHRIST THE INTERCESSOR

Christ is our ultimate model Intercessor. In fact, He is not just the chief cornerstone Paul points to in Ephesians 2:20, He's the Chief Intercessor. Think about it for a minute. Jesus walked the earth doing good and healing all who were oppressed of the devil (see Acts 10:38).

Jesus also walked the earth praying and interceding. Speaking of Jesus, Hebrews 5:6-7 (NKJV) tells us, "'You are a priest forever according to the order of Melchizedek'; who, in the days of His flesh, when He had offered up prayers and supplications, with vehement cries and tears to Him who was able to save Him from death, and was heard because of His godly fear."

Jesus often went up on a mountain by Himself to pray (see Matt. 14:23; Mark 6:46). Sometimes He spent the whole night in prayer to the Father (see Luke 6:12). He was known to get up early in the morning, while it was still dark, and leave the house to find a secluded place to pray (see Mark 1:35). He often slipped away to the wilderness to pray (see Luke 5:16). He prayed in the Garden of Gethsemane (see Matt. 26:36). We see one of the longest prayers in the Bible in John 17, where Jesus prays for His disciples.

Yes, Jesus prayed without ceasing when He walked the earth, fully God and fully man. And after He died on a bloody cross to pay the price for our sin—the ultimate act of intercession—His work wasn't finished. When Jesus rose from the grave and was seated at the right hand of the Father, He didn't stop praying. Just as He prayed for His disciples when He walked the earth, He's still praying for us now. Two Scriptures confirm this reality.

As I write in *The Intercessor's Devotional*, Paul reminds us, "Who is he who condemns? It is Christ who died, and furthermore is also risen, who is even at the right hand of God, who also makes intercession for us" (Rom. 8:34 NKJV). That has always fascinated me. The New Living Translation says He is "pleading for us." *The Message* relates that Jesus is "in the presence of God at this very moment sticking up for us."

If Scripture had pointed this out once, it would have been enough. But Hebrews 7:25 (NKJV) gives us another picture of Christ the Intercessor: "Therefore He is also able to save to the uttermost those who come to God through Him, since He always lives to make intercession for them."

We are never more like Jesus than when we are making intercession. When Jesus hung on the cross, it was the ultimate act of intercession. Jesus intervened on our behalf. Biblically speaking, He who had no sin became sin for us so that we could become the righteousness of God in Him (see 2 Cor. 5:21). But He always lives to make intercession for you. Thanks be to God we have an advocate with the Father—Christ the Intercessor.

UNDERSTANDING TRUE INTERCESSION

In order to stand true as an intercessor, we need to understand what intercession is. An intercessor is one who intercedes. What does it mean to intercede? Interceding is mediating. It's meeting with God for the purpose of petitioning on behalf of others so God will meet their needs. It's an action of intervening on behalf of another.

S.D. Gordon, a prolific author and minister in the 18th and 19th centuries, had a deep understanding that: "Prayer is repeating the victor's name (Jesus) into the ears of Satan and insisting on his retreat." Prayer, then, is a weapon against dark forces that dare to intrude upon God's will in the earth.

Charles Spurgeon, a 19th-century Englishman known as the prince of preachers, put it this way: "True prayer is neither a mere mental exercise nor a vocal performance. It is far deeper than that. It is a spiritual transaction with the creator of Heaven and Earth."

Dutch Sheets, author of *Intercessory Prayer*, wrote these thoughtful words, "I believe our prayers do more than just petition the Father. I've become convinced that in some situations they actually release cumulative amounts of God's power until enough has been released to accomplish His will."[1]

Since we know the enemy counterfeits what God creates—he can't create anything of his own accord as he has no creative power—we can be assured if there is true prayer and intercession, there is false prayer and intercession. So what is true intercession? Well, what's *true*? *Merriam-Webster's Dictionary* defines *true* as: honest, just, legitimate, accurate, without deviation, loyal, and genuine. Jezebel, a false intercessor, hates true intercession.

JEZEBEL HATES TRUE INTERCESSION

True intercession is honest intercession. Honest intercession doesn't try to manipulate God into doing something He doesn't want to do. Honest prayer is free from deception. Honest intercession is sincere intercession, like Moses when he asked God to heal his sister Miriam from leprosy even though she had complained about him and judged him unfairly.

True intercession is just intercession. *Just* means conforming to what is morally upright or good and true. Just intercession is based on the Word of God or inspired by the Spirit of Truth. God delights in the prayers of the righteous because the prayers of the righteous are just (see Prov. 15:8). What's more, the desire of the righteous will be granted (see Prov. 10:24).

True intercession is legitimate intercession. Legitimate intercession is lawful intercession. It's intercession in accordance with the spiritual laws of prayer and the requirements of God. Legitimate intercession conforms to God's principles, rules, standards, and ways. Legitimate intercession succeeds with God. Abraham's cry for Sodom and Gomorrah is an example of legitimate intercession as he appealed to God's nature.

True intercession is accurate intercession. Accurate intercession is free from error and drives specific results. Accurate intercession hits the target rather than praying amiss. Not all intercession is accurate intercession. James explains, "You lust and do not have. You murder and covet and cannot obtain. You fight and war. Yet you do not have because you do not ask. You ask and do not receive, because you ask amiss, that you may spend it on your pleasures" (James 4:2-3 NKJV).

True intercession is loyal. Loyal intercession is unswerving in allegiance to the plans and purposes of God. It's intercession that is in faithful alignment with the lawful sovereign God and His government. Paul was a faithful intercessor who prayed without ceasing for the church. Daniel was a faithful intercessor who prayed three times a day.

THE MARKS OF INTERCESSORS OF LIGHT

Intercessors of light are not hard to recognize. Intercessors of light don't just release true intercession; they model the ways of Christ the Intercessor. So what are the marks of intercessors of light? Intercessors of light are sacrificial, dedicated to standing in the gap, persevering in prayer, merciful, humble in service, discreet, and motivated by love.

Intercessors of light are self-sacrificial. Jesus made the ultimate self-sacrifice when He hung on a cross to pay for our sins. He literally offered His body as a living sacrifice—and so does the self-sacrificial intercessor. The writer of Hebrews says, "But do not forget to do good and to share, for with such sacrifices God is well pleased" (Heb. 13:16 NKJV). Intercession is a spiritual sacrifice acceptable to God (see 1 Pet. 2).

Anna the prophetess is a strong example of a self-sacrificial intercessor. She laid down her life in intercession. She got married at a young age and her husband passed away seven years later. For decade after decade, Anna did not leave the temple. She served God with fasting and prayer night and day (Luke 2:36-37). She literally gave up her life for prayer. She lost her life in Christ and preserved it (see Luke 17:33).

Intercessors of light are dedicated to standing in the gap to which God calls them. They are determined to be the gate in the gap. God said to Ezekiel, "I looked for someone who might rebuild the wall of righteousness that guards the land. I searched for someone to stand in the gap in the wall so I wouldn't have to destroy the land, but I found no one" (Ezek. 22:30 NLT). Intercessors of light stand in the gap.

As I wrote in *The Intercessor's Devotional*, "If you are an intercessor, there's a gap for you to stand in. When you find that gap, you'll be the most effective in your intercessory prayer efforts." When you let your light shine in the gap, the darkness the enemy is trying to bring into a situation simply must flee. Moses stood in the gap to turn back God's anger against Israel more than once.

Intercessors of light are persevering in prayer. George Mueller, a 19th-century Christian evangelist known for building orphanages, once said: "It is not enough to begin to pray, nor to pray aright; nor is it enough to continue for a time to pray; but we must pray patiently, believing, continue in prayer until we obtain an answer." This is persevering prayer.

Paul the apostle put it this way: "Praying always with all prayer and supplication in the Spirit, being watchful to this end with all perseverance and supplication for all the saints" (Eph. 6:18 NKJV).

Intercessors of light have a mercy mindset. Abraham is a strong example of a mercy-minded intercessor. He prayed relentlessly for Sodom and Gomorrah to be saved, even though the city was beyond wicked. And he knew he was pushing it. After pleading with God not to destroy the city for the sake of 50, then 40, then 30, then 20, he said, "Let not the Lord be angry, and I will speak but once more" (Gen. 18:32 NKJV).

Intercessors of light offer humble service, expecting nothing in return. They do not intercede to gain the applause or rewards of men. They intercede to serve the King of kings and Lord of lords. They are especially effective because they walk in wisdom in intercessory prayer realms because wisdom comes to the humble (see Prov. 11:2). Humility rewards them with grace to pray more (see James 4:6). God highly esteems their work and promotes them in the spirit (see 1 Pet. 5:6).

Intercessors of light are discreet. As I write in *The Intercessor's Devotional*, "As intercessors, we need to master the art of discretion. God may show you things about people that He doesn't want repeated to anyone. He just wants you to stand in the gap and agree in prayer for His will in their life. Likewise, people may share intimate details of their struggles with you, hoping you will pray. You need to keep it confidential."

Intercessors of light are love-motivated. In fact, intercession that is not motivated by love is not motivated by God because God is love (see 1 John 4:8). God so loved the world that He sent His only begotten son to make intercession on the cross—and still charges Him with interceding from His position in glory.

Intercessors of light, when they mature, become intercessors of love. They are patient in intercession and kind enough to pray for those who accuse them and abuse them. They don't boast about the breakthroughs but give glory to God. They are not proud but humble, not resentful of the hours in intercession but rejoicing to be used of God.

THE LIGHT OF THE WORLD

Christ-called intercessors are intercessors of light because Jesus is the light of the world. When intercessors follow Jesus, they will not walk in darkness but will have the light of life (see John 8:12). We need to continually guard the light and life we carry because the enemy comes to steal, kill, and destroy (see John 10:10).

Intercessors, we are supposed to walk as children of light (see Eph. 3:8). When we get hurt and wounded—when people influenced by the flesh or the devil harm our souls—darkness has an opportunity to find a place in our minds. That darkness attracts evil spirits, including Jezebel. When you are hurt and wounded, run to Jesus because Jezebel is lurking.

Get in the Word. His Word is a lamp to your feet and a light to your path so that you don't enter Jezebel's territory or allow her to enter yours (see Ps. 119:105). Jesus said the one who walks in darkness does not know where he is going (see John 12:35). The entrance of His Word brings light when you are confused by what you are walking through (see Ps. 119:30).

Even when darkness attacks you, you can let your light shine. The light in you, Jesus, will overcome the darkness attacking you. The devil's darkness cannot overcome the light within you (see John 1:5). The Lord is your light and your salvation, and you don't have to fear the darkness or Jezebel (see Ps. 27:1).

The enemy wants to give you a black eye and flood you with darkness. Jesus warned, "The lamp of the body is the eye. Therefore, when your eye is good, your whole body also is full of light. But when your eye is bad, your body also is full of darkness" (Luke 11:34 NKJV). Keep your eyes on Christ the Intercessor, who is your light, and you will not succumb to the darkness. You will not fall prey to Jezebel's intercessors—or become one.

Remember, satan is the fathers of lies (see John 8:44). God is the father of lights (see James 1:17). Jezebel wants to turn your light into darkness. Jezebel wants to turn you to the dark side of intercession. Jezebel wants to turn your intercession from blessing to cursing. Jezebel wants to use you and will wound you to tempt you into unforgiveness and bitterness. Choose to be a burning and shining lamp for God. Choose to be an intercessor of light who keeps the fire on the altar burning.

I'm reminded of a poem by the Scottish writer Robert Lewis Stevenson called "The Lamplighter." The poem is about a man named Leerie whose job is to light lamps as the sun sets. He walks around with a ladder, climbing up to lift the lid and to light every lamp in the city so no one has to walk in darkness. Intercessor of light, when you pray you are releasing Christ's light into situations.

We need to shine like the Centennial Bulb, which is the longest burning light bulb in history. It's been burning since 1901. How is a mystery! It was first installed in a fire department hose cart but went on to enlighten several different fire stations over the years. It has shone for over one million hours. So go ahead and burn and shine like John the Baptist.

PRAYER TO PRAY IN THE LIGHT

Father, in the name of Jesus, help me to walk in Your light. Help me to walk in Your life. I don't want to walk in the light the world gives as that is not true light. I want to walk in Your divine light that exposes darkness as I stand in intercession.

I don't want to walk in a counterfeit light. I want to walk in Your supernatural light that leads me and guides me into revelation. I don't want to walk in New Age light. I want to walk in biblical light that illuminates my prayer path. Jesus, You are the light of the world. I love Your light.

Help me walk in the light so the blood of Jesus cleanses me from all unrighteousness. I want to proclaim Your marvelous light in the nations. I want others to see my light and come to Jesus. I want to walk as a child of light into the prayer territories into which You've called me. Make me burn and shine.

NOTE

1. Dutch Sheets, *Intercessory Prayer* (Bloomington, MN: Bethany House, 1996), 38.

CHAPTER 3

INTERCESSORS OF
DARKNESS

A blind man went to visit his friend in the next village. It was night when he set out to return home. The blind man's friend gave him a lighted lamp as he bid him farewell. The blind man wouldn't take the lamp, saying, "I don't need this lamp, dear. I will use my stick to find my way. Nights and days are similar to me."

But his friend urged him, saying, "Keep it with you. It is not for you, but for others. If you carry this lighted lamp with you, others can see it. Then they will not collide with you."

The blind man started his journey carrying the lighted lamp with him. On the way, there was a storm. He waited under a tree and resumed his journey after the storm passed. Suddenly a stranger coming in the opposite direction collided with him and both of them fell to the ground.

The blind man shouted angrily, "Couldn't you see the lighted lamp in my hand, man? Are you blind?"

The stranger replied, "I am not blind but your lamp was not burning."

"I am sorry, dear," said the blind man. "I am blind and did not know that the flame was put off by the storm."

What's the lesson on this story? Dr. Babu Philip, a former professor at the Cochin University of Science and Technology in India who wrote the story, offers this insight: "We boast that we are the chosen children of God and that His grace will protect us from all evil. But the divine light shining in us gets extinguished by our sinful actions and then we may fall. Let us consciously guard the lamp of God shining in our hearts. It will illuminate us and enlighten everyone around us."[1] Amen!

MY AHA MOMENT

Both the Queen Jezebel we read about in 1 and 2 Kings and the false prophetess Jezebel we read about in Revelation 2 committed repetitive sinful actions. First John 3:4 (ESV) offers this truth: "Everyone who makes a practice of sinning also practices lawlessness; sin is lawlessness." Jezebel's intercessors operate in a lawless spirit that works in darkness and wants to darken the hearts of Christ's intercessors of light.

Although I have written several books dealing with various aspects of the Jezebel spirit, I had never heard anything about Jezebel's intercessors. Of course, we see Jezebel's prophets in the Bible. They ate at Jezebel's table. They were her yes-men. They were on her payroll. Since all prophets are intercessors, it only makes sense that if there are Jezebelic prophets there are Jezebelic intercessors.

However, the initial revelation of Jezebel's intercessors didn't come to me through study. The revelation of Jezebel's intercessors came to me by the Spirit while I was teaching in my School of Prophecy. Flesh and blood did not reveal this to me. The Holy Spirit opened my eyes to this dark reality out of the blue. It was a sudden aha moment that I expounded upon right there in the class. There are false intercessors in the Body of Christ, and much of the time they are Jezebel's intercessors.

In my class, I said by inspiration of the Holy Spirit: "There are those who espouse themselves to be intercessors but they are nothing more than gossipers. They never pray about a thing, they just want the information. They are Jezebels in disguise. Jezebel is an information-seeking spirit. They are not seeking the information so they can pray and see God intervene. They are seeking information to prey—P-R-E-Y—on your hurts and wounds. All intercessors are not pure-hearted or true. Some of them have false agendas."

Think about it. It only makes sense, doesn't it? We see a lot of warnings in the Bible about false gifts—and intercession is a gift. While we are all called to intercede, some have a gift of intercession. So if there is true intercession, there is false intercession. Indeed, you can't read a single book in the New Testament that doesn't warn about deception or falsity, and we'd do well to heed these warnings and cultivate the fear of the Lord in our lives.

WARNING OF FALSE GIFTS

I want you to see this—really see this. While the Old Testament has an enormous amount to say about false prophets, the New

Testament focuses on a variety of falsities in the church. When you observe the volume of these warnings, it should cause you to drop to your knees and pray for discernment to escape the snare of deception. Deception tends to trap those who are hurt, wounded, haughty, rebellious, or ignorant of the Word.

John warned against false spirits, which would include Jezebel: "Beloved, do not believe every spirit, but test the spirits, whether they are of God; because many false prophets have gone out into the world" (1 John 4:1 NKJV). Paul echoes this warning and says, "Test all things; hold fast what is good" (1 Thess. 5:21 NKJV). Again, Paul warned "Abhor what is evil. Cling to what is good" (Rom. 12:9 NKJV). And again, "Stay away from every kind of evil" (1 Thess. 5:22 NLT). We're supposed to discern between good and evil.

Jesus warned of false prophets. In Matthew 7:15-16 (NKJV), "Beware of false prophets, who come to you in sheep's clothing, but inwardly they are ravenous wolves. You will know them by their fruits." Jesus also warned about false christs: "For false christs and false prophets will rise and show signs and wonders to deceive, if possible, even the elect" (Mark 13:22 NKJV). I wrote a lot about false prophets in my book *Discerning Prophetic Witchcraft* and the two sequels, *Exposing Prophetic Witchcraft* and *Deliverance from Prophetic Witchcraft*, so I won't go deep into the fruit of false prophets and false prophecy here.

Peter warned of false prophets and teachers:

> *But there were also false prophets among the people, even as there will be false teachers among you, who will secretly bring in destructive heresies, even denying the Lord who bought them, and bring on themselves swift*

destruction. And many will follow their destructive ways, because of whom the way of truth will be blasphemed. By covetousness they will exploit you with deceptive words; for a long time their judgment has not been idle, and their destruction does not slumber (2 Peter 2:1-3 NKJV).

Peter warned about false teachers.

For when they speak great swelling words of emptiness, they allure through the lusts of the flesh, through lewdness, the ones who have actually escaped from those who live in error. While they promise them liberty, they themselves are slaves of corruption; for by whom a person is overcome, by him also he is brought into bondage (2 Peter 2:18-19 NKJV).

Paul warned about false apostles. "For such are false apostles, deceitful workers, transforming themselves into apostles of Christ" (2 Corinthians 11:13 NKJV). John warned about false pastors:

But a hireling, he who is not the shepherd, one who does not own the sheep, sees the wolf coming and leaves the sheep and flees; and the wolf catches the sheep and scatters them. The hireling flees because he is a hireling and does not care about the sheep. I am the good shepherd; and I know My sheep, and am known by My own (John 10:12-14 NKJV).

Paul warned about false Christians more than once:

> *Yet not even Titus who was with me, being a Greek, was compelled to be circumcised. And this occurred because of false brethren secretly brought in (who came in by stealth to spy out our liberty which we have in Christ Jesus, that they might bring us into bondage), to whom we did not yield submission even for an hour, that the truth of the gospel might continue with you* (Galatians 2:3-5 NKJV).

Second Corinthians 11:26 also calls out danger from "false brethren." If there can be false brethren, there can be false intercessors.

Jesus warned against Jezebel, the false prophetess.

> *Nevertheless I have a few things against you, because you allow that woman Jezebel, who calls herself a prophetess, to teach and seduce My servants to commit sexual immorality and eat things sacrificed to idols* (Revelation 2:20 NKJV).

I shared these examples because you need to be convinced of the reality that anything that God does, the enemy mimics, counterfeits, or otherwise perverts. So while there is no explicit Scripture about false intercessors in the Bible, what I mentioned earlier bears repeating: All intercessors are not prophets, but all prophets are intercessors. If there are false prophets, there are false intercessors. Beyond that, we know there are people who pray with self-centered, carnal, or even wicked motives. That's called false prayer.

FALSE INTERCESSORS DON'T START OUT FALSE

I've always said false prophets don't start out as false prophets, if they were ever prophets at all. Many times, prophets turn to the dark side because of the lust of the flesh, the lust of the eyes, and the pride of life (see 1 John 2:16). It's the same with intercessors.

The lust of the flesh concerns ungodly desires that appeal to our carnal appetites. The lust of the eyes are external attractions that drive covetousness. The pride of life is the desire to be platformed, famous, and puffed up. These temptations are common to man, but the enemy works overtime to tempt those who can damage his kingdom the most. That category includes prophets and intercessors.

Most intercessors don't start off serving Jezebel, unless perhaps Jezebel got to them before Christ did. Keep this in mind: When people enter the Kingdom of God by faith in Christ, they are not automatically delivered from every emotional woe any more than they are healed of every bodily sickness. Just as people who have cancer before salvation may still have cancer after salvation, believers can get saved and still be under the influence of a Jezebel spirit. In that way, they can be Jezebel's intercessors from the start.

However, more often I see true intercessors move to the dark side through hurts and wounds. Yes, some fall to the lust of the flesh, the lust of the eyes, and the pride of life. But many avoid all those snares only to be hurt and wounded in the church by people who misunderstand them, reject them, and even persecute them. Intercessors are ripe for Jezebel's picking if they are not deeply rooted and grounded in the love of Christ.

In my experience, those who call themselves intercessors usually start out as sold-out, on-fire prayer warriors. Jezebel intentionally wounds them so she can woo them. If successful, they come under Jezebel's protection. Their personalities are morphed. Their prayer and intercession changes. And they become agents of darkness in the church, doing more harm than good with their prayers.

JEZEBELIC INNER VOWS

Jezebel loves to collect intercessors like trophies because she hates to see the will of God come to pass. Think about it. It only makes sense for the enemy to pollute intercessors so they cannot pray with purity and see the answers to their petitions.

One way Jezebel defiles Jehovah's intercessors is with an insidious strategy called inner vows. An inner vow is a promise we make to ourselves when we're angry or in pain. Inner vows often start with the words "always" or "never," such as: I will never ask anyone for help. I will never let anyone control me. I will never share my innermost thoughts. I will never receive a compliment. I will never go out at night. I will never marry again. I will never be responsible for the actions of another.

We often make inner vows as children or when some great harm comes to us. We may forget all about the words we spoke, but the vow is still intact. Here's the problem: Inner vows invite demons to come and protect us. That's why we manifest when someone triggers the wound that sparked us to make the inner vow. The demon is influencing our thoughts. When we make an inner vow with Jezebel, we give our mind over to her way of thinking in certain areas.

JEZEBEL ALMOST GOT ME!

Let me share with you my "almost" inner vow story. I was part of an abusive apostolic church at the time. It was beyond militant. It was near cult-like in many respects. The ministry was holding a School of the Prophets, which I paid to attend. However, my daughter had an event one Saturday and I needed to keep my commitment to her, so I chose to skip the class. After the event we went out to eat. When my daughter and I came out of the restaurant, there was a message on my phone from the house prophet.

In a commanding voice, she said, "I know you feel that devil coming up because it's ready to come out. I know you are nauseous because of the influence of the demon. You need to hurry and get here to church so we can cast this out of you." Well, that was shocking. Nothing could have been further from the truth. I had a great day with my daughter. I was not at all nauseous. The message made me angry, but I also got hit with witchcraft. I didn't understand the spiritual implications at the time. I was just pure mad!

My daughter and I went home and we took a nap. I was in a deep sleep when the house prophet started knocking on the door to my condo. It woke my daughter up and she came in to tell me the prophet was at the door. I did not invite her to my home, nor did I welcome her in. I thought it was beyond aggressive. When we didn't answer the door, she called the phone. I did not answer. She left a message on the phone berating me.

She was citing Scriptures like Proverbs 3:34 (ESV), "Toward the scorners he is scornful" and Proverbs 24:9 (NASB), "The scorner is an abomination to humanity" and Proverbs 13:1 (NASB), "A wise son accepts his father's discipline, but a scoffer does not listen to rebuke." Then she hung up. This released more witchcraft, but it also hurt my feelings. This woman was my mentor. I couldn't believe she would say those things. Everyone knew I was at an event with my daughter. But this Jezebelic church wanted to control me. When they could not control me, Jezebel set out to wound me.

After hearing that message, I climbed back up in my loft bed and felt sorry for myself. I cried. I was really hurt. I stewed on her words until I finally heard a voice that said, "I will never let them hurt me again." The voice was startling. I knew it wasn't me and I knew it wasn't the still small voice of the Lord. I had never been taught anything about inner vows. I never even heard about inner vows. But the Holy Spirit within me knew what was going on.

Instinctively, I rose up out of my bed and shouted, "No!" What I didn't know then that I know now is this: It was Jezebel's voice trying to seduce me. It was the voice of a wicked power trying to get me to release an inner vow so that Jezebel could be my protector and make me an intercessor of darkness. And that's how quickly it happens. I arose, forgave those who hurt me, and moved on. Forgiveness is a key to avoiding darkness.

The late John Loren Sandford in his excellent book *Deliverance and Inner Healing* wrote, "There may be areas in which our outer person thinks we have forgiven others—especially those most formative to us in childhood—but counsel and prayer reveal that such forgiveness is far from complete. It may be that coping mechanisms from childhood are still causing us to act and react in childish ways (see 1 Cor. 13:11). Or bitter roots may have sprung back to life, causing us to defile others and reap harmful consequences that we cannot, without counsel, even explain."[2]

My experiences with Jezebelic intercessors and other intercessors of darkness are why at Awakening Prayer Hubs, a prayer movement focused on revival, awakening, and the final harvest (www.awakeningprayerhubs.com), we offer an inner healing track for intercessors. Many come in wounded from other churches and other movements. They just want to pray, but they've been compromised. If they don't get healed, they are targets for Jezebel that can do damage to what God is building.

QUALITIES OF DARK INTERCESSORS

Dark intercessors, or false intercessors, carry certain qualities, whether we discern them or not. Let's look at the deep and lengthy definition of *false* in *Merriam-Webster's Dictionary* to get some clues as to the qualities of dark intercessors. *False* means "not genuine, intentionally untrue, adjusted or made so as to deceive, intended or tending to mislead, not true, not faithful or loyal, lacking naturalness or sincerity, inaccurate in pitch, threateningly sudden or deceptive, treacherous."

This is dangerous for the church and dangerous to the intercessor. In Isaiah 29:15-16 (NLT), the Lord says:

> *What sorrow awaits those who try to hide their plans from the Lord, who do their evil deeds in the dark! "The Lord can't see us," they say. "He doesn't know what's going on!" How foolish can you be? He is the Potter, and he is certainly greater than you, the clay! Should the created thing say of the one who made it, "He didn't*

make me"? Does a jar ever say, "The potter who made me is stupid"?

Some dark intercessors know exactly what they are doing. They purposely stand in the way of God's will. They don't genuinely care about the cause. Their motive is dark. They set out to deceive.

Speaking of the end times that we're in right now, Paul wrote, "But evil men and impostors will grow worse and worse, deceiving and being deceived'" (2 Tim. 3:13 NKJV). They are treacherous, which means likely to betray your trust. Their intercession is marked by hidden dangers, hazards, and perils. But make no mistake, they shall be ashamed who deal treacherously without a cause (Ps. 25:3). That's why we need to pray for their deliverance.

SEEING THE DARKNESS IN US

It's hard to see in the dark, and it's hard to see darkness in us. Have you ever been in a hotel room only to wake up in the middle of the night and bump into a wall trying to find the bathroom? Dark is dark and, again, it's not just hard to see in the dark. It's hard to see the dark in us. We need to be careful not to try to remove the speck that is in our brother's eye when we have a beam poking out of our own eye (see Matt. 7:3). Jesus offered these wise words:

> *Your eye is like a lamp that provides light for your body. When your eye is healthy, your whole body is filled with light. But when it is unhealthy, your body is filled with darkness. Make sure that the light you think you have is*

not actually darkness. If you are filled with light, with no dark corners, then your whole life will be radiant, as though a floodlight were filling you with light (Luke 11:34-36 NLT).

Darkness is deceptive. If we could see it, we would cry out for deliverance. So what do we do? We need to examine ourselves and test ourselves (see 2 Cor. 13:5). Paul was pulling wisdom from Lamentations 3:40 (NKJV) in his words to the church at Corinth that still speak to us today: "Let us search out and examine our ways, and turn back to the Lord."

Apart from Christ we can do nothing (see John 15:5). We can't even examine ourselves without first inviting His light in to probe our souls. The nature of deception is that we don't know what we don't know, and we can't see what we can't see. David put it this way: "Who can understand his errors? Cleanse me from secret faults" (Ps. 19:12 NKJV). That's why he cried out, "Search me, O God, and know my heart; try me, and know my anxieties; and see if there is any wicked way in me, and lead me in the way everlasting" (Ps. 139:23-24 NKJV).

We can't repent for and renounce something we don't see. As I always say, an enemy exposed is an enemy defeated. Allow the Lord to test your heart. You don't want any common ground with darkness. You don't want any false spirit informing your intercession. Pray like David, "Examine me, O Lord, and prove me; try my mind and my heart" (Ps. 26:2 NKJV). If He shows you something, repent and rejoice as you break free.

By the same token, sometimes it's hard to see the dark in others. That's because sometimes darkness hides, which is why it needs to be exposed. That demands discernment. If we have common ground with darkness, one of two things may happen: We will point fingers at others when we should be pointing a finger at ourselves. Or we will not see the darkness in others because we are blind to it.

"God is light and in Him there is no darkness at all" (1 John 1:5 NKJV). All things become visible when the light exposes them (see Eph. 5:13).

Our goal is to see people turn away from darkness to light and from the power of Jezebel to God (see Acts 26:18). God delivered us from the domain of darkness when we accepted Christ, and we are told to have no part in the unfruitful works of darkness, but rather to expose them (see Eph. 5:11). We need to get the darkness out of our hearts so we don't fall prey to Jezebel. Just as God separated light from darkness in Creation, He's still working to separate light from darkness in people with the truth that sets us free. Ask Him to separate darkness from you and to separate dark intercessors from your midst if they do not want to pursue freedom.

In the next chapter, we are going to talk about why Jezebel's intercessors are so dangerous. I will warn you, what you will read in the next chapters will disturb you. It will also open your eyes to the very present danger.

PRAYER

Father, in the name of Jesus, help me to follow You. You tell us in Your Word that whoever follows Jesus will not walk in darkness. So help me follow Jesus in all my ways for all my days. Help me to see any areas of my life where I am not following You wholeheartedly, completely, with all sincerity and with full abandon.

Father, I don't want to be a hypocrite. I don't want to be one of Jezebel's puppets in prayer. I don't want to present a form of godliness while denying Your true power. Help me turn away from anything that hinders love. Show me any secret sins in my soul that I cannot see so I can quickly repent and turn my heart completely back to You.

Forgive me for all the times I did not obey Your Word or Your Spirit when I knew the right thing to do. Forgive me for all the times I did not pray when You led me to. Forgive me and cleanse me from all unrighteousness for Your glory. Cleanse me from the darkness. Make my eye single. Dispel the darkness. I want Your light and life to show through me. Free me from every evil thing and let Your face shine upon me and give me peace.

NOTES

1. Dr. Babu Philip, "A Light for the Night," Christian Moral Stories, April 22, 2010, https://christian.moral-stories.com/2010/04/light-for-night-blind-man-went-to-visit.html.

2. John Loren Sandford, *Deliverance and Inner Healing* (Grand Rapids, MI: Chosen Books, 2008), 56.

CHAPTER 4

WHY JEZEBEL IS ATTRACTED TO INTERCESSION

She was quiet when she first came into the house of prayer. She was steadfast in attendance, but she kept to herself. She was often found lying on her face in quiet intercession. She appeared to be a laid-down lover. Despite her shy demeanor, though, she was one of the noticeable intercessors. And, as it turned out, her demure persona was purposeful.

Her name was Holly and she loved to pray. She positioned herself as a forerunner, a messenger to houses of prayer. She was at Awakening House of Prayer (AHOP) for every meeting, large or small. She seemed to carry wisdom in intercession. What we didn't know was that she was both wise and harmful as a serpent. But the Jezebelic influence in her intercession was hard to discern because of her storyline.

See, Holly came to us from another prayer ministry—a large prayer ministry. She had credentials. She had references. We knew some of the same people and had the same passion to see revival, or so I thought. Because she came highly recommended, when she emerged from what we thought was her "shell" and started praying from the mic we thought she was an answer to prayer. In reality, she was a combatant to our prayer.

Indeed, she was Jezebel's intercessor in disguise. She was operating in stealth for months. No one saw the spirit influencing her. At least not at first. No, not until she had woven her wicked web of witchcraft in the prayer meetings, drawn people to herself, and rooted down deep into our leadership culture. This was one of the most cunning, manipulative Jezebelic intercessors I've seen to this day because her shroud was holiness.

When we finally discerned Jezebel's influence in her life and gently confronted it, she cried and turned the tables on us. Rather than admitting she had a problem so that she could receive inner healing ministry and deliverance from childhood wounds, she made us the problem. She holed up in one of our facilities and refused to leave for months. Finally, like Jehu, we had to throw her down—almost literally. We had to evict her from the premises.

JEZEBEL THE DICTATOR

Right after we evicted Holly, another one of Jezebel's intercessors came in to AHOP. This one, we'll call her Amy, had recently left a megachurch ministry. Like Holly, Amy had a strong intercessory prayer anointing. She seemed to inspire intercessors to go deeper and longer in prayer. But she started controlling the prayer meetings when I was on travel assignments.

Amy, for example, refused to let certain people pray, not because they were compromised but because they posed a threat to her leadership. In other words, they could see the spirit that was influencing her and she knew it. So she cut off their voices in prayer just like Queen Jezebel cut off the prophetic voices in the Old Testament. Pretty soon, our prayer community dwindled down to Amy and her groupies.

Amy got what she wanted. Full control. Amy started demanding her groupies purchase specific books and read them. She did this using authority I did not give her. I never knew anything about the books until a woman in our community approached me about Amy asking her to join the intercessory prayer team and giving her a list of required books. Amy wasn't just operating in a wrong spirit. She was operating in a Jezebel spirit, which was dangerous as it sought to wound pure intercessors through rejection.

DEMANDS FOR POSITION

Right after Amy was exposed, refused correction, healing, and deliverance, and left the ministry, the third of Jezebel's intercessors came in undercover. We'll call her Maggie. Maggie was older, wiser, and less noticeable. Maggie was a seasoned intercessor and at times seemed to pray in the atmosphere of heaven. But she was attracted to intercession because she was power hungry and seeking position.

Maggie wanted to be my number two. She wanted to preach while I was traveling. She wanted to be an apostle. When the Holy Spirit gave me a detailed dream showing me the spirit in which she was operating, I started backing up. When she saw she wasn't going to get what she wanted, she left AHOP, insisting the Holy Spirit told her to sit at home for a year and worship Him privately.

Let me be clear on this point: Anyone can come under the influence of a Jezebel spirit, even for a moment. Jesus handpicked James and John, but one day they listened to the voice of another spirit. In judgment they wanted to call down fire from heaven to consume the Samaritans (see Luke 9:54). Jesus corrected them for operating in the wrong spirit. Thankfully for them, they didn't manifest and go all over Israel slandering Jesus like many do when they are confronted for operating in under demonic influences.

Likewise, Jesus personally called Peter to walk with Him. Jesus even gave Peter a new name (he formerly went by Simon). But right after Peter received the revelation that Jesus was the Christ he had the audacity to pull Jesus aside to rebuke Him (see Matt. 16:22). Jesus didn't receive Peter's correction. Instead, Jesus rebuked him for seeing things from a human point of view rather than God's point of view (see Matt. 16:23). Peter stayed the course and became a great figure in Christianity.

The Jezebel spirit is dangerous because it is ultimately looking to hijack prayer. Jezebel knows one of the best ways to do that is to hijack intercessors. So she looks for open doors in our souls and enters them. What better place than at a prayer meeting?

JEZEBEL'S IMPURE MOTIVES

Remember, a Jezebelic intercessor is an intercessor who has been compromised by the Jezebel spirit. Holly, for example, had been molested as a child and had deep father wounds on top of mother wounds on top of sibling wounds. And the incense from those unhealed, festering soul wounds attracted Jezebel to hijack what otherwise could have been an impactful prayer ministry. Again, any intercessor can come under Jezebel's influence—and it doesn't have to be a pain as deep as sexual abuse. The rejection intercessors continually face is enough to open a door.

Once Jezebel infiltrates an intercessor's thinking, their motives are no longer pure. That's one problem—and it's a real one. But the other side of this Jezebelic coin is the compromised intercessor doesn't usually realize they are compromised because they are deceived. They may actually believe they are doing what is right—and it can be hard to convince them otherwise. Nevertheless, we are accountable for our actions even if Jezebel is driving them.

Scripture is clear about the fruit of impure motives or self-deception about what is right and wrong. Proverbs 16:2 (NIV) says, "All a person's ways seem pure to them, but motives are weighed by the Lord." Jezebel's intercessors are often praying with wrong motives. Ironically, selfish motives hinder our prayers. And James 4:3 (NIV) says, "When you ask, you do not receive, because you ask with wrong motives, that you may spend what you get on your pleasures." But that wrong motivation can also lead to witchcraft prayers.

JEZEBEL LOVES THE INCENSE

Jezebel is attracted to the realm of intercession and wants to be anywhere with the prayers of the saints—which are the incense that fill up the golden bowls in heaven until they finally tip over (see Rev.

5:8). Jezebel attacks the pure at heart to turn them into eunuchs who pray her will.

Jezebel especially targets intercessory prayer leaders. In fact, I can't tell you how many intercessors I promoted to a position of authority at AHOP in the early days, only to have them fall prey to this spirit. I've learned well that you have to make sure prayer leaders are healed before you install them into a position. If they have any common ground with Jezebel, it won't be long before you have more than a mess on your hands.

JEZEBEL NEEDS GOSSIP FUEL

Jezebel's intercessors love intercession because she can find pain points to prophesy into by listening closely to the prayers of others. Armed with an understanding of the needs or woes of a person or a church, she can better position herself to come in like a knight in shining armor and meet those natural and spiritual needs.

Jezebel's intercessors love intercession because they overhear juicy bits of information that fuel their gossiping spirit. Jezebel often uses what was prayed to cast aspersions on the leaders, on the church, or those in authority. If someone is praying for the salvation of your family, it won't take long for Jezebel to spread a rumor around the church that your household is not in order.

Jezebel, like satan with Jesus in the wilderness, will quote Scriptures such as, if a person wants to be an overseer, he must be "one who rules his own house well, having his children in submission with all reverence" (1 Tim. 3:4 NKJV). Soon, the true intercessors are seeing a compromised and unfit-to-lead pray-er. Jezebel is at work, poised to come in and replace the leader. We must see through the gossip and shut it out.

Jezebel loves intercession because she likes to meddle in other peoples' affairs. Gossip is device of the devil and, as Paul the apostle said, we must not be ignorant to the devil's devices (see 2 Cor. 2:11). Gossip and meddling seem to go hand in hand. While a gossip is someone who has a habit of sharing personal information about other people (which can lead to harmful rumors), meddling is interfering without a right or inserting oneself into affairs that are none of one's business.

PARTNERING WITH THE SPIRIT OF GOSSIP

Psychologists say gossipers are insecure cowards who feel empowered when they spread rumors. According to psychologist Dr. Ned Hallowell, there's a kind of emotional sadism that's rooted in gossip, especially if it's negative. "People tend to take pleasure in someone else's misery and delight that it's not happening to them," he says, referring to such gossip as a sort of "safe, vicarious sadism."[1]

Psychology aside, gossipers can attract a spirit of gossip that drives them to meddle into other people's business and, in doing so, forward the enemy's plans to steal, kill, and destroy (see John 10:10). Gossip, which includes slander, rumors, dishing the dirt, backbiting, and planting negative seeds about people, is a work of the flesh and is in the realm of witchcraft.

It's important to understand what the Bible says about gossiping and meddling. Consider the strong language the Bible uses: "Don't spread gossip and rumors" (Lev. 19:16 MSG). "And the women also who serve the church should be dignified, faithful in all things, having their thoughts set on truth, and not known as those who gossip" (1 Tim. 3:11 TPT). "A twisted person spreads rumors; a whispering gossip ruins good friendships" (Prov. 16:28 TPT). "That you also aspire to lead a quiet life, to mind your own business, and to work with your own hands, as we commanded you" (1 Thess. 4:11 NKJV).

These are just a few of the many Bible verses on gossiping and meddling. If you are the victim of gossip, the first thing you need to do is remember you are not wrestling against flesh and blood (see Eph. 6:12).

Even if it's just a work of the flesh and not a spirit of gossip, you can be sure the enemy is inspiring the work of gossipers and meddlers. In order to take authority over the attack, you first need to forgive the evildoer. Harboring unforgiveness in your heart just opens the door wide to more enemy attacks.

Next, confront the spirit of gossip that has targeted you. Bind the spirit of gossip in the name of Jesus. Ask the Lord to forgive those who are gossiping about you, and return good for their evil (see 1 Pet. 3:9). Moving in the opposite spirit sets you up for God's vindication in your life.

Another female pastor in my region was gossiping about me. Her gossip, as gossip always does, got back to me. I was angry at first because, as female pastors, we should really be supporting each other. Religious spirits love to attack us and we need to stand together. I couldn't believe she would stoop so low as to spread lies about me. Instead of getting into the flesh, though, I sent her a gift—an autographed copy of my book on revival—and told her we need to pray for each other. Then I invited her to lunch. She never responded, but that broke the back of the gossip attack. She never put her mouth on me again.

On a more personal front, don't take the words of gossip to heart. Know who you are in Christ and don't take another thought to the gossip. If the gossip doesn't stop, you may eventually have to confront the gossiper. If you do, confront them with Scripture. Speak the truth in love from a place of forgiveness. Tell them what the Bible says about gossip and let the Holy Spirit bring the conviction.

JEZEBEL'S FALSE SPIRIT OF COUNSEL

Jezebel loves intercession because she loves to counsel people. Jezebel's intercessors will take information gained in the prayer meeting to start counseling and advising those who are going through trials and tribulations. After the prayer meeting, she will approach the hurting privately with a prophetic word or an offer to pray with them every day. Earlene did this with a young woman in the church who had a seer gift but massive emotional issues.

In fact, Earlene puffed her up about her giftings and offered to pray with her five mornings a week. In doing so, Earlene formed a soul tie with the young woman and eventually turned her against our ministry. When Earlene was exposed and asked to leave the church, the young woman came to us confessing that she felt something was off and asked us to help her break those soul ties and the witchcraft. But within six months, the young woman decided to follow Jezebel (Earlene) out of the church to learn about the love of Jesus.

JEZEBEL WANTS TO RULE THE ROOST

Jezebel loves intercession because she wants to rule the roost. If anyone has a touch of Jezebel's influence on their life, they will seek to be in control—or at times even dominate. It may start with dominating a conversation, but that's not where it will end. Jezebel's intercessors want to be seen as the go-to person with authority to make decisions. Jezebel walks in illegitimate authority. Remember, the Queen Jezebel exerted illegitimate authority over the prophets, killing them. She exerted her illegitimate authority over Naboth, having him murdered. She is power hungry—and that's an understatement.

Jezebel will cross boundary lines and speak out of turn, wanting to appear to have clout where she doesn't have any. This causes confusion in your prayer group as she tells people one thing when the truth is often entirely contrary.

Jezebel wants to be the head intercessor because in this role she has the greatest opportunity to influence others. If she can't be the head intercessor, she will cozy up to the head intercessor hoping to receive delegated authority through faithful service. Jezebel's intercessors will offer to help where help is desperately needed. They'll do anything to be close to the leader.

I can't tell you how many intercessors I have promoted to a position of authority only to have them fall prey to this spirit. For a season, it was one after another. I finally spoke to a friend of mine about the issue, and he said he had the same problem. Here's how he solved it: He decided he was the head intercessor. I did the same thing and that ended my drama.

JEZEBEL WANTS TO BE PLATFORMED

What do I mean by platformed? Jezebel's intercessors want the microphone, or they want leadership of the prayer meeting. Jezebel thinks more highly of herself than she ought. She thinks she's invincible and can talk her way out of anything because she's a master manipulator. This is a chameleon spirit with many faces. Jezebel's intercessors often shapeshift when exposed.

Look at this. When Jehu came riding, Jezebel did not hide. She was so arrogant she thought she could seduce him. When she couldn't seduce him she threatened him. Second Kings 9:30-31 (CEV) reads:

> *Jehu headed toward Jezreel, and when Jezebel heard he was coming, she put on eye shadow and brushed her hair. Then she stood at the window, waiting for him to arrive. As he walked through the city gate, she shouted down to him, "Why did you come here, you murderer? To kill the king? You're no better than Zimri!"*

Let's unpack this for a minute. Jezebel wasn't hiding. She had set herself up in a high place—on her platform in the royal palace—looking down on him. She wanted to be seen. Many early Bible commentators say she was trying to seduce Jehu, hoping to maintain her queenship under his new founded rule of kingship. She thought she could control him like she did Ahab. Arrogant.

Pulpit Commentary writes, "Jezebel, trusting in the charms and the fascination which had been so potent over Ahab, may have imagined that she had still enough beauty left to capture Jehu, provided she increased her natural attractions by a careful use of all the resources of art."[2]

When Jezebel saw that her seducing tactics weren't working on Jehu the way they did on Ahab, she started launching false accusations against him. Zimri was someone who had killed a king and then committed suicide. She's basically saying, "Killing me will be suicide for you."

People with a Jezebel spirit want visibility. They want to be the center of attention. That's one reason why they like to prophesy. People love to receive prophetic words and Jezebel will oblige. In Revelation 2:20, Jesus said that woman Jezebel called herself a prophetess. Catch this. She had followers who believed she was a prophet and thought her prophetic words were true.

The church in Thyatira gave Jezebel a platform and that's what she wanted. But she was teaching them heresy. She was pointing them to other gods. Many in the church at Thyatira didn't discern it. They were following a false prophet rather than the leader of the church. And guess what, Jesus rebuked the lead pastor of the church for allowing Jezebel to seduce these people with her false prophecy and false teachings. He should have stood against it. Instead, he put up with it.

Again, Jesus said in Revelation 2:20 (NLT), "But I have this complaint against you. You are permitting that woman—that Jezebel who calls herself a prophet—to lead my servants astray. She teaches them to commit sexual sin and to eat food offered to idols." Again, the leader of the church was allowing it. Don't tolerate Jezebel.

JEZEBEL THRIVES ON INFORMATION

Jezebel loves intercession because she thrives on gathering inside information. Jezebel wants to be in the inner prayer circle because she wants to understand the problems and challenges the church or the leadership is facing. But she also seeks information about other intercessors, so she understands their weak points. When Jezebel understands your pain or insecurities, she can exploit them.

You've heard it said, "Knowledge is power." Jezebelic intercessors are information-seekers because the knowledge they have about people gives them power over people's reputations and emotions. This insider information makes them appear to be close to leadership or somehow "in the know." Jezebel also spreads false information based on perverted revelations, often accusing people in authority of walking in sin.

JEZEBEL WANTS PROXIMITY

Jezebel loves intercession because it gives her proximity. Demons who work through people affect you most when they have proximity. *Proximity* just means close. While Jezebel is a principality, once this spirit can infect someone's soul Jezebel has boots on the ground so to speak. The person can gain proximity to intercessory prayer groups and do Jezebel's dirty work in the earth through people.

Remember, demons are persons without bodies. To be most effective in the earth, demons need bodies. Put another way, demons need to influence or occupy the souls of people in order to possess the legal right to operate in the earth. Just as Jesus had to be born of a woman and walk in flesh and blood doing miracles, signs, and wonders, demons are most effective when they are operating through people to steal, kill, and destroy (see John 10:10).

Let's think of this practically. Your demonized coworker would never be an issue for you if you worked at another company. The demonized coworker would not have proximity. They couldn't set you up for failure or gossip.

JEZEBEL LOVES TO PROPHESY

Jezebel is attracted to intercession because she loves to prophesy and teach—and intercessors are often hungry to learn. Remember, Jezebel is a false prophet and false teacher who seduces. Prayer meetings are prime time to release prophecy. Jezebel uses false prophecy to draw people to herself. Her goal is to set herself up as a voice in your life, and then manipulate you.

In his excellent book *Spiritual Warfare*, Richard Ing addresses this demonic phenomenon: "Jezebel loves to prophesy because it is a way of manipulating people. 'Thus saith the Lord' is a powerful tool used to manipulate the saints and the leaders. After all, who dares to disobey God? ...Jezebel often prophesies in church. If she can get close to the prophet or pastor of the church, she will then be able to influence the leaders about what the church should do. She will erode the vision of the church and its efforts to stay on the narrow path."[3]

John Robertson, in his book *Winning the Battles in Spiritual Warfare*, wrote this about Jezebel: "Her visions will be vague, ambiguous and mystical in the sense that they can be so generalized that they can be interpreted in many different ways; they may even sound spiritual in nature, but requiring of her interpretation for application. Some people are so desperate for a prophetic 'word,' regardless as to whether it is actually from the Holy Spirit or if it is soulish, that they will chase or pursue her for prophetic utterances."[4]

JEZEBEL LOVES TO TEACH

Jesus said in the Book of Revelation that Jezebel teaches and seduces (see Rev. 2:20). Jezebel's intercessors love to teach and seduce the saints for several reasons. First, she wants to draw people to herself in a private group. Second, she wants to renew their minds to her perverted way of thinking, twisting Scriptures and defying the authority of what church leadership is teaching.

Ing writes, "She wants to be the head priestess in the church. She often has her own group of intercessors or Bible class at her home. She draws the sheep to her, and they begin to adore and hang on her every word. Then, she subtly makes negative remarks about those in leadership to erode their power."[5]

Some years ago one of Jezebel's intercessors came into the church and prophesied, "The Lord wants me to start a Bible study about the end times in my home." I told her home groups were not part of our vision in this season. She insisted, "The Lord said...." I told her strongly, "Well, the Lord did not say that to me, and this church is under my stewardship." Nevertheless, she was drawing people to herself behind the scenes. She had people giving her money, running her errands, and bringing her food.

JEZEBEL WANTS TO BE ADMIRED

Jezebel's intercessors love to pray because it's an opportunity to display their eloquence, their knowledge, their "intimate" relationship with Jesus, and their eloquence in prayer. Indeed, Jezebel loves to impress you with her intercession. But make no mistake: Jesus is not impressed. I know this because I've read Christ's words in Luke 18:9-14 (NKJV):

> *Also He spoke this parable to some who trusted in themselves that they were righteous, and despised others: "Two men went up to the temple to pray, one a Pharisee and the other a tax collector. The Pharisee stood and prayed thus with himself, 'God, I thank You that I am not like other men—extortioners, unjust, adulterers, or even as this tax collector. I fast twice a week; I give tithes of all that I possess.'*
>
> *"And the tax collector, standing afar off, would not so much as raise his eyes to heaven, but beat his breast, saying, 'God, be merciful to me a sinner!' I tell you, this man went down to his house justified rather than the other; for everyone who exalts himself will be humbled, and he who humbles himself will be exalted."*

JEZEBEL HAS A RELIGIOUS SPIRIT

Remember, Jezebel has a religious spirit. The Queen Jezebel was very religious indeed. She served the gods of Baal and Ashtoreth with fervor. Religious spirits are nefariously nasty. Religion is a murdering spirit. People in bondage to religious spirits murdered Jesus, Stephen, the apostles—and want to murder you. They may not crucify you, stone you, or behead you, but these self-righteous serial killers have you on a spiritual hit list. They will assassinate your character and massacre your reputation if you refuse to submit to their ridiculous, irreligious rules.

The spirit of religion is a murderous spirit that seeks to heap condemnation on the saints. Religion sets up rules that no one can keep perfectly; it's a legalistic spirit that works to strip you of your true identity as the righteousness of God in Christ Jesus and weigh you down with guilt and condemnation or, on the other hand, pride.

One of the earmarks of the religious spirit is hypocrisy. *Merriam-Webster's Dictionary* defines a hypocrite as "a person who puts on a false appearance of virtue or religion." The story of the woman caught in the act of adultery is a good example of the religious spirit. The scribes and Pharisees brought Jesus a woman caught in sin—in the very act of adultery. They wanted to see her stoned and asked Jesus what He had to say about it (see John 8:1-5). Of course, they didn't drag the man alongside her to be punished. Hypocrisy.

I've discovered most of us have religious mindsets about something or another. So we need to check our own hearts and motives above all—and when we see a person operating in a religious spirit, we need to be wise as serpents and harmless as doves (see Matt. 10:16). Sometimes we're called to confront it like Paul did with

Peter, but most of the time we're called to our knees to ask God to break through their religious mindset with His light.

PRAYER

Father, in the name of Jesus, would You purify my motives. I want to love intercession because I love the Chief Intercessor, Jesus, and when I stand in intercession I am serving His purpose in the earth. Help me see and renounce any false motives and break any common ground with Jezebel. Grace me so I can rightly discern the Jezebel spirit operating through others and stand against it.

NOTES

1. Jennifer Lea Reynolds, "Rumor Has It: Why People Gossip and How You Can Cope," Psychology Today, March 4, 2021, https://www.psychologytoday.com/us/blog/human-kind/202103/rumor-has-it-why-people-gossip-and-how-you-can-cope.

2. BibleSoft, *The Pulpit Commentary*, s.v. 2 Kings 9:30, (2010), https://biblehub.com/commentaries/pulpit/2_kings/9.htm.

3. Richard Ing, *Spiritual Warfare* (New Kensington, PA: Whitaker House, 1996), 53.

4. John Robertson, *Winning the Battles in Spiritual Warfare* (Bloomington, IN: WestBow Press, 2013), 369.

5. Ing, *Spiritual Warfare*, 53.

CHAPTER 5

WHY JEZEBEL'S INTERCESSORS ARE SO DANGEROUS

During the Apostolic Council of Prophetic Elders—a roundtable of prophets under Cindy Jacobs' leadership—I was talking with Dr. Sharon Stone in between prophetic strategy sessions. Based in Windsor, England, Dr. Sharon is a pioneer of prophetic ministry in Europe. She's been there for decades laboring for a pure prophetic movement and has seen great success.

I told Dr. Sharon, "I'd really like to start going to London once a month to train people in the prophetic and build houses of prayer." This had been a vision of mine since 2016, but there had been fierce opposition to me executing on the desire the Lord put on my heart. Two years later, I still hadn't taken action. But Dr. Sharon spurred me on.

Specifically, she said, "I know. You told me that before. You should start right away." Right away? I thought she meant six months down the road, with proper planning and deep intercessory prayer covering.

I asked her, "What do you mean by right away?"

She said, "Now!" That was mid-November. We started going to London in January.

Our first School of the Prophets was packed to the brim. We had the help of a woman we knew who lived in Croydon (South London). She found the facility. She helped get the word out. It was so easy. So much grace! Or so we thought. We didn't first discern that this lady, we'll call her Cathy, was Jezebel's intercessor in disguise.

With the success of the first meeting, we went back again and worked with Cathy, whose Jezebelic tendencies were still undercover. The second meeting was a fiasco. We had less than half the attendance. We discerned there was sabotage from the inside. We couldn't put our finger on it, so we kept praying and asking the Holy Spirit to expose the saboteur. When we went back the third time, Jezebel manifested openly through Cathy.

Suddenly, massive witchcraft was hitting both me and Vanessa, the one the Lord assigned to travel with me to plant houses of prayer and train hungry believers in the prophetic. Strife was trying to creep in. In the meeting hall, I pulled Vanessa in a back room. I told her I would not get up and preach until we resolved what felt like strife between us. In that conversation is when we realized the woman was one of Jezebel's intercessors and had been releasing witchcraft against us with word curses.

Not ironically, while we were in the back room trying to clear the air, Cathy literally was praying division over us. When I say literally, I mean publicly from the microphone. We walked in on

Cathy praying about how Vanessa and I were divided and how we needed to find unity. I took the microphone and shut it down—then shut her out.

In this last chapter, I shared with you why Jezebel loves intercession. Jezebel uses intercession as a way in and then, later, as a weapon of mass destruction for your prayer group, ministry, or business. Jezebel's intercessors are dangerous because their motives are anti-Christ and anti-Kingdom. With that in mind, let's look more specifically at why Jezebel's intercessors are so dangerous.

JEZEBEL IS A FALSE PROPHET IN DISGUISE

We talked about how Jezebel loves to prophesy, but it goes beyond releasing prophetic words—or even prophetic curses. Jezebel's intercessors carry a false prophetic spirit and use prophetic words to divide and conquer. Jezebel's intercessors come to you in sheep's clothing but inwardly they are ravenous wolves (see Matt. 7:15). This false prophetic spirit has many consequences of which we need to be aware.

Jesus said in Matthew 24:24 that false prophets will arise and lead people astray. Jezebel's intercessors will lead people away from their first love. They will lead people away from His heart. Jeremiah 23:16 tells us false prophets fill us with vain hope. Jezebel's intercessors puff and prop people up, prophesying positions on the worship team or increase in their lives where God has not spoken. Jeremiah 14:14 says false prophets prophesy lies in God's name. You can't believe a word Jezebel's intercessors say. They breathe lies. They twist truth.

Let me give you a practical example: When one of our leaders was out of church for a few weeks, Jezebel's intercessor started prying for information. She asked people close to the woman where she was under the pretense of concern. Desperate for knowledge, she started looking at the obituaries in the newspaper only to find out the woman's husband had passed away. She claimed the Holy Spirit told her about the death, but clearly she was stalking the obits for information. It was beyond sickening.

Ezekiel 13:9 says false prophets see false visions. Micah 3:11 tells us false prophets are money motivated. Jeremiah 23:13 tells us false prophets prophesy by a false god. Jeremiah 23:26 tells us false prophets prophesy out the deceit of their own heart. Jezebel's intercessors have many faces and many tactics, but their motive is the same—to seduce in order to control.

One of the ways Jezebel does this is through compelling pity and prophetic flattery. One of Jezebel's intercessors pulled a younger woman under her wings. Jezebel was praying with her every morning on the way to church—and her target grew more and more emotionally unstable with every prayer. Jezebel positioned herself as the woman's spiritual mother and committed to being there for her all hours of the day and night—something our church leadership could not practically do. Eventually, Jezebel convinced the woman—and her husband—into letting her charge a new big screen television on their credit card. She promised to pay this young couple back. Guess who's still paying for the big screen television?

JEZEBEL INTERCESSORS HAVE A POLITICAL SPIRIT

Remember, Queen Jezebel's marriage to Ahab was political in nature. Jezebel is not motivated by love but by power and politics. Jezebel had a political spirit. If you want to know what a political spirit looks like, just look at Christians manifesting on social media during election seasons. But the political spirit isn't just political about politics.

Jezebel's intercessors often have a political spirit that's subtle. Someone with a political spirit always needs an enemy. Someone with a political spirit demonizes people they don't agree with. Someone with a political spirit is competitive and performance driven. Someone with a political spirit gets angry when others try to discuss the other side of an issue. Someone with a political spirit flows in manipulation and intimidation.

Are you getting the idea? In the aftermath of the 2020 election, we lost about 50 prayer hub leaders because they let the political spirit overtake them. They weren't content with praying for spiritual awakening, which was the vision. They wanted me to lead the charge and have rallies and get political. I would not do that because that's not our vision. God told me not to do it. So they turned on me and tried to kill the movement. I'd rather have a small movement that's pure than a large movement where Jezebel uses me like a puppet. Yet God rebuilt Awakening Prayer Hubs and we are in dozens of nations.

JEZEBEL INTERCESSORS RELEASE WITCHCRAFT PRAYERS

Any Christian can tap into witchcraft prayers, and perhaps not the way you think. I'm not talking about releasing word curses, incantations, spells, and potions. Witches are not the only ones who release witchcraft prayers. A Christian who is praying to God in the name of Jesus can release a witchcraft prayer without knowing it.

So what is a witchcraft prayer? Simply put, a witchcraft prayer is when you pray your own will instead of God's will. Witchcraft prayers are not Spirit-led but flesh-led. You could call them fleshly prayers or carnal prayers, but I call them witchcraft prayers because that's what this type of intercession is releasing.

Witchcraft prayers aim to control people and situations. Rather than trusting God to bring His will to pass, we assert our will into the mix. Even if you are praying God's will, you can't tell God how to do His job. We'll talk more about witchcraft prayer in a later chapter. I want you to become savvy at discerning these destructive intercessions.

JEZEBEL'S IS ON A SEEK-AND-DESTROY MISSION

Jezebel's intercessors work to seek and destroy what God is building. Consider the words of Christ in John 10:10 (NKJV), "The thief does not come except to steal, and to kill, and to destroy. I have come that they may have life, and that they may have it more abundantly."

Catch that. The enemy has a threefold ministry. All demons have the same agenda—to steal, kill, and destroy. Different demons go about accomplishing this mission in different ways. Fear works differently than rejection, for example. Jezebel's intercessors are working to obstruct the work of prayer and intercession.

One way Jezebel's intercessors seek to destroy the work of God is, as mentioned, through witchcraft prayers. But Jezebel's intercessors also work outside the realm of prayer to steal, kill, and destroy from their position as one who prays without ceasing for the church.

Consider the chronicles of Nehemiah. Nehemiah was a type of an apostle, but he was also an intercessor. Nehemiah 1 is almost entirely his intercessory prayer to God on behalf of Israel after he heard the wall in Jerusalem was broken down. After Nehemiah got the king's permission to go rebuild the wall, he almost immediately faced interference from false workers like Sanballat, Tobias, and Geshem. The obstacles were incessant.

This trio of false intercessors pretended to be concerned for the welfare of Babylon. They were angry when they heard about Nehemiah's plans to rebuild the wall. These false Babylonian intercessors continued harassing Nehemiah.

BEWARE DURING THE BUILDING

In the first year of AHOP, I encountered a trio of false intercessors. All three initially presented as sold-out, on-fire intercessors with a passion to build the house of prayer. But soon enough, all three manifested their true intentions—to distract the builders from

God's work. These deceived intercessors may not even realize they are on an assignment from the evil one.

The first false intercessor came in with a commitment to pray five days a week. That lasted about a month before the truth manifested. When impure motives came to the light, leadership called him out. That's when this Jezebelic intercessor took his mask off and began persecuting, bringing false accusations, and calling down God's judgment. He tried to rally others to his side, but God frustrated his purposes, and he faded out as quickly as he appeared on the scene.

The second false intercessor came in with the line, "You need me! You can't do this without me!" She was faithful to pray and even help with administrative work in the beginning. But soon enough she began criticizing the model and the leadership. The false accusations were much more subtle, laced with feigned sincerity, but they were accusations nonetheless. This Jezebelic intercessor left for another prayer ministry she felt could bring her more recognition.

The third false intercessor was almost identical. She came in with a commitment to pray five days a week. She never did fulfill that commitment. It was a lot of talk and inconsistent action, along with a critical, presumptuous spirit. When corrected, the false accusations came flowing in against leadership. When those accusations went unanswered, this spirit influenced her to "declare war" and demand a position in the house of prayer.

We also see false intercessors hindering the work of the rebuilding of the temple in the Book of Ezra. Ezra 4:1-5 (NIV) reads:

> *When the enemies of Judah and Benjamin heard that the exiles were building a temple for the Lord, the God*

of Israel, they came to Zerubbabel and to the heads of the families and said, "Let us help you build because, like you, we seek your God and have been sacrificing to him since the time of Esarhaddon king of Assyria, who brought us here."

But Zerubbabel, Joshua and the rest of the heads of the families of Israel answered, "You have no part with us in building a temple to our God. We alone will build it for the Lord, the God of Israel, as King Cyrus, the king of Persia, commanded us."

Then the peoples around them set out to discourage the people of Judah and make them afraid to go on building. They bribed officials to work against them and frustrate their plans during the entire reign of Cyrus king of Persia and down to the reign of Darius king of Persia.

JEZEBEL'S INTERCESSORS BRING DEFILEMENT

Jezebel's intercessors defile pure intercessors. *Defile* means to make unclean. It means to corrupt or debase. It means to violate the purity. In order to ascend to the holy hill in prayer, intercessors need clean hands and a pure heart (see Ps. 24:3-6). When Jezebel's intercessors defile other intercessors, it's like a virus that quickly spreads through the group.

Jezebel defiles intercessors by planting evil seeds in their soul against the leadership or through flattery and tapping into their insecurities. They may pray eloquently, but their words outside of prayer are clearly not Spirit-inspired. Jezebelic intercessors are defiled and corrupted because they are compromised.

Jesus said in Mark 7:21-23 (NLT), "For from within, out of a person's heart, come evil thoughts, sexual immorality, theft, murder, adultery, greed, wickedness, deceit, lustful desires, envy, slander, pride, and foolishness. All these vile things come from within; they are what defile you."

JEZEBEL MASTERS DISTRACTIONS

Jezebel's intercessors are a major distraction to the real work of prayer because they are often dominating drama queens who take prayer off into directions the Spirit is not leading. Or they cause so many issues in the church, business, or prayer group that the prayer leaders have to spend more time praying over how to handle the Jezebel than they do other critical matters at hand.

We had one Awakening Prayer Hub leader who turned her prayer hub meeting into personal prayer time for her and her failing businesses. Others reported her. We had another prayer hub leader who decided to focus all their prayer on dog rescue. Someone else reported her. We had another prayer hub leader who decided to start an inner healing ministry under our banner and was drawing people to herself for personal freedom.

These Jezebelic intercessors don't last long in our movement because we know how to root them out through prayer. An enemy exposed is an enemy defeated. We are a movement of intercessors who understand honor and love the anointing. Anything that interrupts that flow is quickly discerned and dealt with in a spirit of reconciliation.

JEZEBEL'S DISCREDITS TRUE INTERCESSORS

Jezebel's intercessors will point out the flaws in true intercessors and try to cause you to question their prayers or discredit their motives. *Discredit* means to cause disbelief in the accuracy or authority of someone. It is an attack on someone's reputation. It's an attack that seeks to disgrace—or cause you to lose grace in the eyes of others.

In the early days of Awakening House of Prayer, one of Jezebel's intercessors worked overtime to discredit one of my leaders. Darla's father had just passed away, so she was unable to be as present as she once was. Darla was dealing with estate issues and grieving at the same time, making it difficult for her to keep up with some duties.

While the rest of us rallied around Darla, Jezebel's intercessor took the opportunity to discredit her in an effort to take her position. Jezebel's intercessor was pointing out all of Darla's mistakes and insisted she wasn't fit to serve on the leadership team. She positioned it as an act of mercy for Darla to step down and, of course, she offered to step into that position. I saw what was going on and gave a flat "no."

Nehemiah dealt with this. As soon as he had rallied workers to rebuild the wall around Jerusalem, he met with opposition that sought to paint him as a rebel: "But when Sanballat the Horonite, Tobiah the Ammonite official, and Geshem the Arab heard of it, they laughed at us and despised us, and said, 'What is this thing that you are doing? Will you rebel against the king?'" (Neh. 2:19

NKJV). Take note of how he dealt with their accusations, though, in verse 20 (NKJV): "So I answered them, and said to them, 'The God of heaven Himself will prosper us; therefore we His servants will arise and build, but you have no heritage or right or memorial in Jerusalem.'"

Know this: If you set out to expose Jezebel's intercessors, they will turn on you, work to discredit you, put scandalous words in your mouth that you never said, cast evil aspersions on you, paint you as a Jezebel, and more. Like Nehemiah, your heart posture must be toward God. You have to trust the God of Heaven will defend your character and prosper you as you continue to put your hand to the plow He assigned you. Jezebel's intercessors will have no right or memorial in your work.

JEZEBEL WANTS TO MAKE EUNUCHS

Jezebel loves intercession because she's looking for disciples. Jezebel makes eunuchs out of young intercessors. The word *eunuch* comes from the Hebrew word *caric*, which means "to castrate."

Although Jesus made it clear that some eunuchs made a conscious decision to become eunuchs out of their own free will for the Kingdom of God's sake (see Matt. 19:12), Jezebel's modern-day spiritual eunuchs don't fall into this category. Jezebel is on a mission to spiritually castrate the saints—especially prophets and intercessors—and keep them under her thumb. Jezebel wants to make disciples who have no power.

Biblically speaking, eunuchs were often found in the households of kings, particularly to work in women's bedchambers. Eunuchs, for example, were appointed to keep the harem of virgins for King Xerxes (see Esther 2:3). Eunuchs were permitted to work in female bedchambers because they had essentially been emasculated. We know there were eunuchs in Jezebel's household (see 2 Kings 9:32).

There is plenty of information online about Jezebel and her eunuchs but not a lot of scriptural backing for the revelations. Some like to say eunuchs are Jezebel's spies, students, or spiritual children, but there's no evidence of that in the Bible. These anecdotal descriptions can lead people into error as they pursue a witch hunt for Jezebel's eunuchs.

One clear role of a eunuch as laid out in Scripture in relation to Jezebel is an attendant (2 Kings 9:32). In this way, Jezebel's eunuchs were her servants. These eunuchs worked for Jezebel's comfort. Practically speaking, they knowingly serve Jezebel's purposes either because they want to or because they are seduced and deceived. In other words, eunuchs are aligned with Jezebel—sometimes by choice and sometimes by fearful duty—and may execute her evil wishes.

Think about it for a minute. Serving in someone's bedroom puts you about as close as you can get to a person and gives you access to intimate details of their life. Some modern-day eunuchs thrive on this close relationship with seductive Jezebel. Others are trapped through their own insecurities and fears—they need Jezebel because they don't know who they are in Christ. Either way, we need to learn to rightly discern Jezebel's eunuchs in our midst.

I knew a woman who served as Jezebel's eunuch. Maggie was the church administrator with the delegated authority she craved. The Jezebelic pastor told her she could go anywhere they went, so she had intimate details of their lives that gave her a greater sense of worth and elitism. Maggie was essentially serving in Jezebel's bedchamber. She worked overtime to make this Jezebelic pastor look good—even at her own personal expense—because she was seduced by a thimbleful of power he gave her.

It may have been a eunuch who delivered the fearful curse to Elijah that sent him running into the wilderness hoping to die after defeating the false prophets at Mount Carmel. Motivated by fear or a need for acceptance, Jezebel's spiritual eunuchs are at her beck and call. Eunuchs are essentially Jezebel's spiritual slaves.

In the modern-day church, eunuchs aren't physically castrated. They are spiritually castrated. In other words, they may appear to have some spiritual authority in a church setting, but in reality they've been stripped of their spiritual strength to resist the wiles of Jezebelic personalities because they are deceived. I should mention that modern-day spiritual eunuchs don't always serve the leadership. Sometimes they are ruled by Jezebelic church members working to erect their own power structure within the church.

THE WALKING DEAD

Do remember that terrible show *The Walking Dead*? The series features survivors of a zombie apocalypse who are trying not to get attacked by the walking dead. If they are bitten or scratched, they turn into a zombie. This reminds me of Jezebel's intercessors. They want to infect you with a deadly virus that changes you.

Jezebel is looking for disciples just like the Pharisees were looking for disciples. Jesus pronounced woe on the Pharisees because they were moving in a wrong spirit. They were working against

Jesus instead of with Him. Jesus said in Matthew 23:15 (CEV), "You Pharisees and teachers of the Law of Moses are in for trouble! You're nothing but show-offs. You travel over land and sea to win one follower. And when you have done so, you make that person twice as fit for hell as you are."

Jesus had some words for those who follow Jezebel:

> *I am going to strike down Jezebel. Everyone who does these immoral things with her will also be punished, if they don't stop. I will even kill her followers. Then all the churches will see that I know everyone's thoughts and feelings. I will treat each of you as you deserve* (Revelation 2:22-23 CEV).

JEZEBEL ISSUES FALSE DOCTRINE

Jezebel issues false doctrine. Revelation 2:24 calls it the depths of satan. The New International Version calls it satan's so-called deep secrets. The New American Standard Bible calls it the deep things of satan. Jezebel is deep, but she's drawing from the wrong well. If you can't recognize it, you will fall prey to it. It can damage your marriage, your money, and your ministry. But Jezebel's intercessors can be very difficult to discern.

That's why 1 John 4:1 tells us to test the spirts to see if they are of God. That's not just in the realm of prophecy, but we also need to see what spirit people are moving in. Jezebel's intercessors are not moving in the spirit of prayer. Jezebel's intercessors are moving in a wicked spirit that's been plaguing the earth for thousands of years. That's why 2 Corinthians 5:16 tells us we should know each other by the spirit. We could also say we should know what spirit people are of.

PRAYER

Father, in the name of Jesus, help me truly understand the danger of Jezebel's intercessors in my midst so I don't fall prey to the wiles of the wicked one. Help me to stay vigilant because the enemy is roaming about like a lion seeking someone to seize upon and devour. Help me to watch and pray and pray and watch and shut Jezebelic spirits out.

CHAPTER 6

PROTECTION, POWER, AND
PRESTIGE

Back and forth she paced with eyes closed tight. From one side of the altar to the other, she marched furiously with arms flailing. Janice offered loud, passionate cries for God's will to come to earth as it is in heaven. She fervently pushed back the darkness for 15 to 20 minutes straight, seemingly without taking a breath.

Indeed, intense was not a strong enough word for her spiritual warfare. Her intercessory prayer activities seemed deeply sincere as tears poured down her face. And she was faithful. Week after week, Janice showed up to make intercession when few others did. In fact, she was one of the first ones to show up and one of the last ones to leave.

But something was off. At first, I couldn't quite put my finger on it. The content of the prayer was accurate, but the subtle spirit was driving theatrics that were not Spirit-led. Don't get me wrong. I am not against demonstrative prayer when it's pure prayer. Fervency is often demonstrated with volume. But I felt like Paul the apostle who took several days to discern the spirit of divination in the servant girl in Thyatira before he cast it out.

Over the course of a few months, severe emotional instabilities started manifesting in Janice. She would pray fiery prayers one minute and lay on the floor in a heap with puddles of tears around her in the next moment. This was not travail. No, she was clearly suffering from agonizing soul pain. It was like Rachel weeping for her children, refusing to be comforted (see Jer. 31:15). No amount of counseling or encouragement resolved the instability, so I continued to pray for a revelation of the root.

Some months later, everything was exposed. Janice was married to the father of her child, but separated from her husband. The marriage was quickly heading for divorce. At the same time, she was secretly fornicating with a man in the church who was addicted to pornography. She cried the way she did because she was having miscarriages and abortions. Her soul was fragmented, and Jezebel was motivating her intercession. She started out with purity but fell prey to the Jezebel spirit.

COULD JEZEBEL BE HIDING IN YOUR MIDST?

Some of the warning signs I'll share in this chapter were subtly operating through Janice. That's why, like Paul, we need Holy Spirit discernment. Keep in mind, you don't have to tick all the boxes describing the Jezebelic characteristics I outline in the pages ahead to conclude someone's intercession is marked by a demonic influence.

By the same token, someone may manifest the characteristics I am about to share and be under an influence other than the Jezebel spirit. The flesh brings enough trouble of its own, and other demons can infiltrate one's soul to shift their intercession away from God's will. As you read through this, I urge you to do so with a heart bent toward discerning the truth that sets people free.

We must examine the fruit. With regard to false prophets—and Jezebel is one of them—Jesus said:

> *Beware of false prophets, who come to you in sheep's clothing, but inwardly they are ravenous wolves. You will know them by their fruits. Do men gather grapes from thornbushes or figs from thistles? Even so, every good tree bears good fruit, but a bad tree bears bad fruit. A good tree cannot bear bad fruit, nor can a bad tree bear good fruit. Every tree that does not bear good fruit is cut down and thrown into the fire. Therefore by their fruits you will know them* (Matthew 7:15-20 NKJV).

Could Jezebel be hiding in your prayer group? How would you know? We need to discern Jezebel's intercessors in our midst, or they will wreak havoc on the prayer ministry, on our businesses, and on every facet of our lives. Remember, Jezebel, like any other spirit, works to steal, kill, and destroy (see John 10:10). Jezebel does this mainly through seduction. But if Jezebel can't seduce you, she will work to overthrow you.

A LEADER'S BEST FRIEND AND WORST ENEMY

Jezebel's intercessors usually work to get as close to the leader as possible. In fact, when the leader is not around, Jezebel's intercessors may insinuate they are close friends with the leader or have some deeper personal connection with the leader than do others. Jezebel wants to give others the impression that she has a special place in the leader's life.

One of Jezebel's intercessors who infiltrated Awakening House of Prayer, my South Florida church, told anybody and everybody that she was best friends with our house prophet. The house prophet, meanwhile, discerned she was off and tried not to engage with her much. Instead, she engaged in prayer for her freedom. But because Jezebel's intercessor purposely followed her around the church asking questions, it gave a visible impression that her claims of closeness were true. All the while, she was discrediting the house prophet behind the scenes.

We see this pattern of cozying up to the leader in 1 Kings. Jezebel's father Ethbaal arranged a political marriage with Israel's King Ahab. The princess in Ethbaal's kingdom in Sidonia became the queen of Israel. She was living in the palace and sleeping with the king, even though they were not in love. You can't get any closer to authority than that.

Why do Jezebel's intercessors want to be close to the leader? There are three overarching reasons: protection, power, and prestige.

JEKYLL, HYDE, AND JEZEBEL

Protection is one of Jezebel's primary motives for cozying up to leaders. Jezebel's intercessors will sacrifice a lot of time praying for the leaders—and much of this is done publicly. Jezebel will do her level best to make sure the leaders—and other people—know she is making intercession for them because they want to be seen as super spiritual and look important. Jezebel is one of the most committed intercessors in the church. She is usually there to pray every time the doors are open.

A protection-seeking Jezebel is not always easy to discern. That's partly because many times Jezebel is praying accurate, powerful prayers and may release genuine prophecies. Sometimes, they truly are praying God's will from their heart. Unfortunately, other times they are operating in witchcraft. Witchcraft prayers, which we'll discuss in another chapter, can sound accurate but can defy the will of God. Familiar spirits can inform witchcraft intercession just like a familiar spirit informed the girl in Thyatira about Paul and Silas' mission.

Indeed, Jezebel's intercessors can be like Dr. Jekyll and Mr. Hyde. Based on characters in a 19th-century novel by Scottish writer Robert Louis Stevenson, Jekyll and Hyde are the alter egos of one person. The novella chronicles Gabriel John Utterson, a legal practitioner who investigates a series of strange incidents involving an old friend, Dr. Henry Jekyll, and a criminal murderer named Edward Hyde. Spoiler alert: At the end of the book, we discover Jekyll transforms into Hyde through some sort of chemical concoction that frees him to live out his darker side. Some intercessors have a dark side, and that dark side is Jezebel. The Jezebel spirit may not manifest through every prayer, but it has sullied the purity of the intercessor.

Always remember, prayer can sound powerful and eloquent, but that doesn't mean it's inspired by the all-powerful God. It may be inspired by another power—the power of witchcraft. Likewise, since Jezebel operates in a false prophetic spirit—in Revelation 2:20 Jesus notes how Jezebel calls herself a prophetess, signaling the prophetic function of this spirit—she will often have on-time revelation that helps the leaders. Again, it may be accurate, but accurate prophecy does not always equate to Holy Spirit-inspired prophecy. We must discern rather than suspect. Suspicion blocks discernment.

Because of her perceived sacrifice in prayer for the ministry, the leader may unknowingly protect Jezebel's intercessors. The leader may not see Jezebel's real motives because of her passion to help. Leaders always need more help than they have, especially in the area of intercession. So when an accusation comes against the Jezebelic intercessor, the leader may not immediately receive it. The leader may have a knee-jerk reaction to protect Jezebel's intercessor. That's because Jezebel usually doesn't manifest in front of the leader.

Indeed, more advanced Jezebels may successfully hide their motives from the leader. They are like groundhogs. When the leader is around, they are on their best behavior. They only manifest their dastardly deeds when the leader is not present. So when people go to the leader with concerns, the leader finds it hard to believe because they've never witnessed that behavior. Meanwhile, everyone else sees it clearly and often.

Hear me, prayer leaders, you need to trust those intercessors who have proven themselves. You need to give heed to their voice and their warning. You need to take their concerns into consideration and into prayer. When you have two or three of your inner-circle intercessors saying the same thing, bringing forth their own examples, and giving urgent warning, please don't ignore them. You'll be sorry you did.

Jezebel's intercessors have varying strategies. Some may hide underground until the right time. They will lay low so they don't draw attention to themselves. They may pray in the prayer meeting and pray well, but they seem unobtrusive. They appear non-threatening. They are not doing anything out of order. These are the ones you need to be especially concerned with because they are drawing people to themselves and out of the ministry covertly.

And remember, sometimes it takes a season to see fruit manifest. When I was growing up, my dad always planted gardens. He taught me how to plant the seeds and cultivate the soil. But it took a while for the vegetables to spring up. And at first, you couldn't tell what was coming out of the ground. It took the fruit some time to mature to the point that it was clearly recognizable. But once you see it, it's undeniable. Many times, it's the same with discerning Jezebel's intercessors.

One of Jezebel's intercessors came to AHOP a few seasons ago. Her name was Gina. She was targeting hurting women and building relationships with them. She would come to all our meetings and remain relatively quiet. But she was clearly spying on how we did things, even taking pictures of our sign-up sheets to get phone numbers. She was giving money to some of the women and handing out handwritten cards to lure them in. The end game was that she and her husband were going to start a ministry down the street so she was seeing how we did things and trying to draw our people in.

When Gina was exposed, she called as many people in the church as she could to cry and pout about it. Despite having more than half a dozen eyewitness accounts of her inappropriate prayer and prophecy sessions in the corner of the church and in the parking lot, she denied the truth. And that's how Jezebel is. They rarely, if ever, acknowledge wrongdoing. (And when they do, it's to take you off guard.)

We must be careful not to be hasty with people or we'll start making false Jezebel accusations based on the trouble the last Jezebel caused. In other words, when you have a prayer or prophetic ministry, Jezebel will be a frequent visitor. We have to guard our own hearts so we don't get jaded and bitter over the damage the last Jezebel caused. We can then be quick to label people as Jezebels and shut out strong intercessors who would be tremendous assets to our ministry but may just have a few rough edges.

A COMMANDING POSITION

As intercessors, God has given us authority over all the power of the enemy. We can command demons to flee when we're submitted to God. Jezebel wants a different kind of command. She wants a command position. She wants prestige. Keep in mind, *prestige* is defined as "standing or estimate in the eyes of people; weight or credit in general opinion; commanding position in people's minds," according to *Merriam-Webster's Dictionary*.

That means Jezebel wants to be seen. When you have close proximity to the leader, you will be seen. Jezebel also wants the platform, as previously discussed. Jezebel wants the attention of the people, like the Pharisees. Again, Jezebel's intercessors often also carry a religious spirit. Jesus warned about pharisaical prayer in the

Sermon on the Mount. Look at Matthew 6:5-7 (NKJV) and you'll see the religious spirit that's often motivating Jezebel's need for a commanding position in people's minds:

> *And when you pray, you shall not be like the hypocrites. For they love to pray standing in the synagogues and on the corners of the streets, that they may be seen by men. Assuredly, I say to you, they have their reward. But you, when you pray, go into your room, and when you have shut your door, pray to your Father who is in the secret place; and your Father who sees in secret will reward you openly. And when you pray, do not use vain repetitions as the heathen do. For they think that they will be heard for their many words.*

Remember when Jehu came riding on his chariot to throw Jezebel down? You would think Jezebel would have hidden, but she sat in a window in the palace looking down on Jehu, almost daring him to come and get her. She painted her face and put on her best robe trying to seduce him. Ahab was dead and she didn't want to lose the queenship. Jehu was king and she probably thought he could just move in with her.

A POWER-HUNGRY SOUL

Like lucifer before the fall, Jezebel is a power-hungry spirit. Lucifer wasn't satisfied with being an anointed cherub. He wanted to take the place of God. He said from his heart, "I will ascend into heaven, I will exalt my throne above the stars of God; I will also sit on the mount of the congregation on the farthest sides of the north; I will ascend above the heights of the clouds, I will be like the Most High'" (Isa. 14:13-14 NKJV).

Jezebel may submit to a prayer leader for a season, but she really wants to be leader. Make no mistake, she's not satisfied with delegated authority. She wants to be the authority. Jezebel may be content with being head intercessor, but she will use that power in ways that serve her wicked agenda rather than the ministry's mission.

Think about it for a minute. Jezebel didn't care about Ahab. This was not a Jacob and Rachel or a Ruth and Boaz love story. No, Jezebel didn't care about Ahab. She cared about gaining power—particularly religious power. Since she couldn't rule Israel, she built an intimate relationship with the one who did. (Noteworthy is the fact that Athaliah, one of Ahab and Jezebel's offspring, ascended to take the throne after their deaths. The spirit of Athaliah takes revenge for Jezebel and is raging in the earth. Check out my book *Jezebel's Revenge: Annihilating the Spirit of Athalia*.)

"We could name many examples of uncontrolled hungers that produced disaster in the lives in which they raged: David's hunger for Bathsheba, Joab's hunger for position, Gehazi's greed for Naaman's gifts, Jezebel's lust for power, Simon's unnatural desire for the Holy Spirit, and Judas' betrayal of Christ for 30 pieces of silver. All their hungers produced nothing but evil," writes *Forerunner Commentary*.[1] Indeed, the common denominator in all these unfortunate stories is demon powers at work to tempt so they can steal, kill, and destroy. Jezebel's intercessors are in a unique position to do serious damage through infiltrating prayer groups.

A FAITHFUL VOLUNTEER

Jezebel comes in offering to help with anything and everything in order to entrench herself in your prayer group. She looks for the voids and fills them, even if it's not a desirable position. She'll do anything to make inroads and find favor with the leader. Jezebel will serve in kid's church, clean the toilets, work the parking lot. She will do anything asked of her with a smile. She seems to be a godsend, but she is devil-sent.

A woman called Ingrid lived down the street from our church—literally five minutes away. Because I was traveling constantly, we needed someone to meet delivery drivers, vendors, inspectors, and the like. She saw our challenge and quickly came to the rescue. Or at least that's what it looked like. She really came in to ruin relationships and position herself as one in authority in the church. After all, not everyone has a key.

Ingrid was a faithful volunteer for years. She was there every time the doors of the church were open. In fact, she got there before the church doors opened to position herself as one who was trusted. Although she was never ordained and was not part of the various ceremonies churches have, people thought she was one of our main leaders. That, of course, is because they were led to believe this lie.

Jezebel wants the recognition, but she also wants to entrench herself in your life, your ministry, your business, or your family. She will literally make herself indispensable, or so she thinks. After Ingrid was confronted and asked to leave the church, we discovered she told many people, "They can never get rid of me. I am involved in everything and do too much to help." Jezebel, or rather Ingrid, was sorely mistaken.

JEZEBEL USURPS AUTHORITY

Jezebel usurps the prayer leader's authority. If Jezebel is not the prayer leader, she wants to be. She won't submit to the prayer meeting's leader. The rebellion may be subtle, but it's there for the discerning. It may look like straying from agreed upon prayer points or praying for longer than allotted. It's little foxes that spoil the prayer vine.

In Awakening Prayer Hubs, we had a woman who would not follow our protocols. We'll call her Abby. She was drawing people to herself, advertising on social media that she was available to be anyone's prayer partner 24/7. We gently told her that is not the purpose of prayer hubs. That the purpose was to pray for the city, not to minister to individuals in the city 24/7 through prayer. She would seem to comply and take the banner down but then put another one up and play dumb.

Abby was also messaging many of the hub leaders and ministering to them over Facebook and e-mail. She was telling people that I had given her authority to do so and that she was about to be promoted in the prayer movement. None of this was true. When Abby was confronted, she acted hurt and started slandering me to other prayer hub leaders. Then she resigned. Before we shut down her prayer hubs email, we looked inside only to find she was using my name and a photo of her and me together to get in with another major prayer movement. Because she used my name, they let her right in.

Leaders have protocols for a reason. If you are going to be part of someone's ministry, you have to follow their protocols. If you can't or won't, you shouldn't be a part.

DIVIDE AND CONQUER

Jezebel works to divide and conquer. Making subtle and seemingly innocent comments about what people are doing (or not doing that they should be doing) is one of this spirit's favorite devices. Jezebel likes to be the bearer of bad news, reporting damning information to leaders—information that is often inflated. Such exaggerated accusations can destroy unity and hinder the intercessory prayer anointing. The opposite of unity is strife. Strife kills the anointing but Psalm 133:1-3 (NKJV) tells us:

> *Behold, how good and how pleasant it is for brethren to dwell together in unity! It is like the precious oil upon the head, running down on the beard, the beard of Aaron, running down on the edge of his garments. It is like the dew of Hermon, descending upon the mountains of Zion; for there the Lord commanded the blessing—life forevermore.*

Of course, Jezebel knows that Scripture well. She also knows Matthew 18:19 (NKJV), "Again I say to you that if two of you agree on earth concerning anything that they ask, it will be done for them by My Father in heaven." Jezebel will divide and conquer in order to gain position, ruin relationships, or just flat-out breed strife and confusion in a prayer meeting. James, the apostle of practical faith, put it this way:

> *But if ye have bitter envying and strife in your hearts, glory not, and lie not against the truth. This wisdom*

> *descendeth not from above, but is earthly, sensual, devilish. For where envying and strife is, there is confusion and every evil work* (James 3:14-16 KJV).

Back in 2016, I was on the road traveling almost every week. I was rarely at the church on Sundays but had a pastor in place to hold down the fort. One of Jezebel's intercessors made it her mission to ring me with a bad report within minutes of the service ending. Every week, she told me how the pastor wasn't following my protocols and the worship leader wasn't on point. She was trying to turn me against my staff. This Jezebelic intercessor ultimately wanted the pastor's position. Instead, she was shepherded out the door.

Some years later, another of Jezebel's intercessors had to be shepherded out the door. Because my foot was broken and three of our senior staff were out of pocket—and because the fire inspector was coming Monday to confirm a key was in the lockbox—I had to send one of our lay leaders to retrieve the key from Sally. Sally, who was operating in a Jezebelic spirit that was highly cloaked, took offense to the innocent request. Our lay leader was struck so hard by witchcraft during the conversation, she later had hard feelings against me for putting her in the line of fire. Jezebel was trying to bring a division between us. It almost worked, but the truth prevailed.

Paul offered several warnings about divisive people. In Romans 16:17-18 (NLT) he wrote, "And now I make one more appeal, my dear brothers and sisters. Watch out for people who cause divisions...Stay away from them. Such people are not serving Christ our Lord; they are serving their own personal interests. By smooth talk and glowing words they deceive innocent people." And again in Titus 3:10-11 (NKJV) he offered, "Reject a divisive man after the first and second admonition, knowing that such a person is warped and sinning, being self-condemned."

SUPER PROPHETIC?

Jezebel can't help but prophesy. Jezebel's intercessors may or may not prophesy during the prayer meeting. It depends on how aggressive is that spirit's hold on the person's soul. At least at the start, Jezebel's intercessors typically work undercover or below your radar to prophesy to members of the group. The goal is to draw people to herself.

Now, remember this: Men can have a Jezebel spirit too! A young man frequented our prayer room on Friday nights. He never prayed at the mic. He kept his head down the entire time. But he would target women in the parking lot. He took advantage of the time when leadership was busy closing up the prayer room to prophesy to anyone and everyone in the parking lot.

In this way, Jezebel is beyond out of order, but Jezebel is not an orderly spirit. Inspired by the Holy Spirit, Paul wrote these words: "Let all things be done decently and in order" (1 Cor. 14:40 NKJV). And again in 1 Corinthians 14:33 (NKJV), Paul insisted, "For God is not the author of confusion but of peace, as in all the churches of the saints." It goes back to protocols. Some churches are looser than others, but know this: Jezebel thrives where apostolic and prophetic authority is lacking.

Let me give you a little friendly advice. If someone who is not part of your church starts trying to prophesy to you in the parking lot, walk away. These are called parking lot prophets. They are trying to get in your head and into your heart. If someone starts trying to prophesy to you during the altar call when we should all be in one accord in agreement with the Holy Spirit, shut it down. It's out of order. It grieves the Holy Spirit.

JEZEBEL CAN DO NO WRONG!

Jezebel cannot be corrected without getting defensive. Jezebel will protect herself by blame shifting. She'll say your instructions weren't clear. She'll say it was someone else's mistake. She may even apologize if the evidence abounds, but she won't change the behavior. She'll just get better at hiding it.

Jezebel won't submit to correction. I've tried to correct Jezebelic intercessors by speaking the truth in love. I've approached them with a humble heart to help them see what they are flowing in so they can repent. I've never seen one come through. Not one. They usually get combative. They accuse you of being the Jezebel. Even if you give them specific examples, they don't think they did anything wrong. Again, sometimes they will apologize and even shed tears, but without true repentance. In other words, they are sorry they got caught but, if given the opportunity, they will continue the behavior.

This is what's called false repentance. Yes, not all repentance is genuine. Paul explains this in 2 Corinthians 7:10-11 (NKJV):

> *For godly sorrow produces repentance leading to salvation, not to be regretted; but the sorrow of the world produces death. For observe this very thing, that you*

sorrowed in a godly manner: What diligence it produced in you, what clearing of yourselves, what indignation, what fear, what vehement desire, what zeal, what vindication! In all things you proved yourselves to be clear in this matter.

True repentance leads to a change in behavior and is willing to bear the consequences of corrective action. True repentance appreciates godly wisdom and counsel and accepts responsibility. False repentance may offer tears and assurances, but typically has an excuse for the offensive behavior. False repentance is wrapped in promises the offender doesn't plan to keep. That describes Jezebel.

ATTENTION-SEEKING STUNTS

Jezebel wants to draw attention to herself. She thrives on attention. She wants to be recognized and praised and will praise herself if no one else will. Paul offers a warning to those who are self-seeking and do not obey the truth but obey unrighteousness—there will be wrath and fury (see Rom. 2:8). This goes along with Jesus' words about throwing Jezebel on a sickbed if she won't repent (see Rev. 2:22).

Jezebel's intercessors make a show of prayer, perhaps by weeping and howling during prayer sets. Other times, Jezebel's intercessors will brag about their prayer exploits and successes. Jezebel's intercessors will take credit for everyone else's prayer breakthroughs. One of Jezebel's intercessors visited us and spoke of how she had fasted for six months during that year. But it was only September. And she did not appear physically to have fasted at all.

Proverbs 27:2 (NKJV) is clear: "Let another man praise you, and not your own mouth; A stranger, and not your own lips." And Paul said, "When people commend themselves, it doesn't count for much. The important thing is for the Lord to commend them" (2 Cor. 10:18 NLT). In other words, Jezebel's intercessors exalt themselves. It's only a matter of time before God humbles them.

PRAYER

Father, in the name of Jesus, would You help me see through Jezebel's stunts, posturing, and nefarious motives to usurp authority in my midst. Help me never to go on a witch hunt but to discern the interactions, presumptions, plots, ploys, and plans of this divisive spirit so I can stand against it rather than agreeing with it. Protect me from Jezebel's wiles.

NOTE

1. John O. Reid, *Forerunner Commentary*, BibleTools.org, https://www.bibletools.org/index.cfm/fuseaction/Topical.show/RTD/cgg/ID/9166/Gehazis-Greed.htm.

CHAPTER 7

PROPHESYING, TEACHING, UNDERMINING, AND DOMINATING

It was open mic night at Awakening House of Prayer. That means anyone can pray from the mic, but we had never seen anything like what we were about to witness. Indeed, it was so bad it caused me to change our protocols on who can pray from the mic.

A woman came up who looked like she belonged in a New Age commune. We don't judge by appearances because we know better. God looks at the heart. But when she prayed, troubling intercession came from the abundance of her heart (see Matt. 12:34). Her intercession was certainly spirit-led, but it wasn't the Holy Spirit who led it.

This woman, we'll call her Whitney, decided to take over the prayer meeting by force—quite literally. She started praying "witchcraft prayers" and quickly proceeded to launch into an unsanctioned prophetic act. She started marching around the sanctuary, urging others to join her. Meanwhile, her husband was using his phone to stream the shenanigans to social media for the world to see.

Thankfully, no one got out of their seat. They all looked at each other in shock. The livestream was stopped and the mic was muted, but she carried on and on prancing back and forth with her eyes closed until one of our staff tapped her on the shoulder. She was startled as if she has no idea what was going on around her. It seemed she was in some sort of demonic trance. The prayer room was closing, and she and her husband left.

Unfortunately, this diabolical duo came back. This troublemaking couple sat in the parking lot during worship praying before our Sunday morning service. I say praying, but it was not holy prayer. You could feel the witchcraft coming in waves. Finally, they came into the sanctuary toward the end of the worship service as if they owned the place and perched proudly in their seats. I had to stop the service at one point and break the witchcraft because it was too thick to tolerate.

I hoped that would be the last time they showed up, but these Jezebelic intercessors were clearly on an assignment and had well-laid plans to disrupt our services with their witchcraft prayers. Each and every time they attended, there was demonic static in the atmosphere. We resolved to try to pray them into freedom, but they didn't want freedom. They had nefarious motives. After much prayer behind the scenes, Jezebel and Ahab moved on to another church.

As I said in the previous chapter, we need to discern Jezebel's intercessors among us. If we don't, they will wreak havoc on the prayer ministry just like Whitney and her husband did. Remember, Jezebel, like any other spirit, works to steal, kill, and destroy (see

Prophesying, Teaching, Undermining, and Dominating

John 10:10). Jezebel's primary thrust is seduction. But if Jezebel can't seduce you, she will work to overthrow you, your family, your business, your ministry, or any other part of your life she can divide and conquer.

I pointed out a few ways to spot Jezebel's intercessors in action in the last chapter. Let's continue down this path. Remember, this is not meant to be a checklist but a picture of ways Jezebelic intercessors can and do operate.

A word of caution: Just because someone behaves poorly in a prayer meeting doesn't necessarily make them one of Jezebel's intercessors. Unruly intercessors could be operating in the flesh or the soul or some other spirit. Likewise, one doesn't have to manifest all these behaviors to be operating in a Jezebel spirit.

It's critical that we identify and deal with Jezebel's intercessors, as Jesus said in Revelation 2:20 (TPT):

> *But I have this against you: you are forgiving that woman Jezebel, who calls herself a prophetess and is seducing my loving servants. She is teaching that it is permissible to indulge in sexual immorality and to eat food sacrificed to idols.*

JEZEBEL LOVES TO PROPHESY

Jezebel loves to prophesy both publicly and privately. If she can't prophesy from a platform, she'll prophesy to people in the parking lot. Remember, Jezebel called herself a prophetess. She wasn't ordained. She wasn't Christ-given. She was not part of the legitimate fivefold ministry. But that didn't stop her.

Because she prophesies prolifically, many believers who can't hear the voice of the Lord for themselves—or who are always after a new word—are attracted to Jezebel's intercessors. Jezebel's intercessors often start out with, "Let me pray for you." But sooner or later they begin to prophesy. Hurt and wounded souls who are desperate for direction begin to lean on them instead of cultivating their own relationship with the Holy Spirit, which is dangerous on many levels.

Honestly, if the Body of Christ would spend more time pursuing Jesus the Prophet instead of every other self-proclaimed prophet, we would be less likely to fall into Jezebel's snare. Jesus said false prophets will arise and deceive many (see Matt. 24:11). Well, false intercessors are rising and deceiving many as well.

What many don't discern is Jezebel's intercessors are not operating in Holy Spirit-inspired prophecy but are operating in prophetic witchcraft. In my book *Discerning Prophetic Witchcraft*, I went in-depth into discerning this practice. In case you haven't read that book (and you should), it's helpful to understand what prophetic witchcraft is. Let me give you my definition.

While prophecy speaks the mind, will, and heart of God for a person, situation, or nation, prophetic witchcraft can oppose the will of God—or at least lead you into a different direction. Prophetic witchcraft taps into a spirit other than the Holy Spirit, who is the spirit of prophecy.

Since the spirit of prophecy is the testimony of Jesus (see Rev. 19:10), prophetic witchcraft can't be the testimony of Jesus—or what Jesus is saying. Prophetic witchcraft is false prophecy, but it's the source of the prophecy that is concerning. It's not soulish prophecy; it's devil-inspired prophecy.

Maybe you have never heard false prophetic utterance firsthand or witnessed the operation of a false intercessor—or maybe you just haven't discerned these false functions yet. Let me assure you, as one who has walked on the front lines of the prophetic and intercessory prayer movements for decades, false prophets, seers, and intercessors are emerging rapidly with manipulative cunning.

False prophets and intercessors appear to the undiscerning eye as genuine, but they are seeking to devour. They seem sincere, but they are sincerely wrong in their motives. It's important to exercise discernment, to examine the fruit rather than being enamored with a spiritual gift or charisma.

As the head of the church and our Savior, we want to hear the Holy Spirit report what Jesus is saying. The spirit of prophecy is the testimony of Jesus (see Rev. 19:10). Jezebel's intercessors are usually not sharing the testimony of Jesus. Instead, they share prophecies that seek to flatter, manipulate, or control you into freely giving your time, money, or loyalty. Prophetic witchcraft can also come from a spirit of divination, essentially a message straight from the enemy's camp. The message may sound like God, but that doesn't mean God said it.

What's so tricky for many people is prophetic witchcraft can be true—false prophetic people can speak accurate words—but that doesn't mean the information originated in God's heart and mind. Familiar spirits and other demons set out to deceive, and sometimes they set the bait for hungry believers. The bait has an ounce of truth but sells them a pound of lies. Remember the girl from Philippi who followed Paul and Silas around proclaiming they were men of God proclaiming the way to salvation? The Acts 16 incident is recorded so we would know someone operating in a demonic spirit can still share a true prophecy.

JEZEBEL LOVES TO TEACH

Jezebelic intercessors don't just use prophecy to draw people to themselves. They use teaching. In the Book of Revelation, Jezebel was a false teaching prophet. But the Bible says she was teaching the deep things of satan (see Rev. 2:24). Jezebel is a heretical teacher.

You may hear Jezebelic intercessors in the service speaking over the preacher, explaining to the person next to them what's wrong with the message, expounding on what the preacher said as if they know better—or even outwardly correcting the pastor during the sermon. Jezebel had a big following in the church at Thyatira because she drew people to herself based on gifts—perverted gifts—rather than character and the quality of the content.

A Jezebelic intercessor who came into our ministry many years ago suddenly decided she wanted to start a Bible study in her house about the end times. I told her that wasn't something we wanted to do in this season. But she insisted the Lord told her to do it. I told her she lived too far away from the church and it wasn't convenient for our congregation. She insisted the Lord told her to do it. I told her she had no parking in front of her apartment. She insisted the

Prophesying, Teaching, Undermining, and Dominating

Lord told her to do it. I told her, "The Lord did not tell me to do it," and that was the final word.

Jezebel is among those Peter warned us about in 2 Peter 2:1 (NKJV):

> *But there were also false prophets among the people, even as there will be false teachers among you, who will secretly bring in destructive heresies, even denying the Lord who bought them, and bring on themselves swift destruction.*

Jezebel's teaching is off. If you don't know Scripture, it may sound right. You may be told you can't comprehend it because it's too deep, but the Gospel is simple and the Bible was written for laymen to understand. Yes, there are deep spiritual truths, but they are not reserved for a special class of teachers. Second Peter 2:18 (NKJV) warns:

> *For when they speak great swelling words of emptiness, they allure through the lusts of the flesh, through lewdness, the ones who have actually escaped from those who live in error.*

Jezebel twists Scriptures to suit her own agenda in the name of being "deep." At the same time, Jezebel will defy the teaching of the leader, subtly undermining the message or accusing the leader of violating Scripture. Remember, Jezebel wants power and authority and will stop at nothing to attain it.

DOMINATING THE INTERCESSORY PRAYER FLOW

Jezebel will dominate and try to control the flow of intercession in a prayer meeting. *Dominate* is a strong word but it's not too strong. *Dominate* means to rule or control. It means to exert the supreme determining or guiding influence on something or someone. It means to occupy a more elevated or superior position.

Remember, Jezebel is not a spirit of control but will use control as a means to an end. If Jezebel's intercessors can't stop or pervert the prayer, they try to dominate and control the flow of it. Jezebelic intercessors will not stay on point with the prayer agenda because they believe they are being led by the spirit to pray about something more important. Jezebelic intercessors will pray so long you are eventually forced to take the mic.

Jezebel will take it upon herself to become the gatekeeper. Gatekeepers are in Scripture and determine who comes in and out. But gatekeepers in Scripture were not self-appointed. Again, Jezebel appoints herself.

JEZEBEL THE CRITIC

One of the Jezebelic intercessors who came through our ministry was so haughty in her prayer that she criticized everyone else who prayed. Once, she didn't think the person opening the service was praying strongly enough and looked at me and asked, "Do you want me to go pray next?" I knew what she was getting at and I told her no.

Jezebel has a critical spirit, but she usually disguises her criticism with concern. Criticism is "the act of criticizing usually unfavorably," according to *Merriam-Webster's Dictionary*. The very definition of criticize is to find fault.

Criticism is rooted in pride. Discernment is rooted in humility. The critical person points fingers and finds fault because nothing a person does is as good as what they do, how it should be, or how someone else does it.

Criticism is often based on insecurities, offenses, hurts, and wounds. Remember, Jezebelic intercessors are usually deeply hurt and never received the Lord's healing.

Let's continue to contrast criticism with discernment, lest we become critics. Critical people call out things that don't align with their personal preferences or feelings or criticize because they are jealous or just because they don't like someone. Discernment has no personal preference. Discernment prefers the truth. Criticism is often connected with gossip and slander. Discernment is typically quiet. Criticism is purely negative without anything good to say. Discernment is unbiased and neutral.

Jezebel's intercessors often set themselves up as judge. Jesus is the judge. James 4:11-12 (NKJV) warns:

> *Do not speak evil of one another, brethren. He who speaks evil of a brother and judges his brother, speaks evil of the law and judges the law. But if you judge the law, you are not a doer of the law but a judge. There is one Lawgiver, who is able to save and to destroy. Who are you to judge another?*

UNDERMINING LEADERSHIP AUTHORITY

Jezebel's intercessors operate in witchcraft, which is a counterfeit authority. They seek to undermine the leader's authority while appearing to the leader (and others) to support the vision. Jezebel used Ahab's signet ring to have a man set up and murdered. We don't know how many times she did things in his name, but I doubt it was only one time. She also slaughtered the prophets of Jehovah.

Elliot's Commentary explains: "The use of the seal—ordinarily worn or carried on the person—implies Ahab's knowledge that something is being done in his name, into which he takes care not to inquire."[1] And *Jameison-Fausset-Brown Bible Commentary* shares, "Ahab passively consented to Jezebel's proceeding. Being written in the king's name, it had the character of a royal mandate."[2]

Cambridge Bible for Schools and Colleges offers, "She was the real ruler, he only king in name. The letters would be prepared for her by the royal secretaries. Jezebel's part was to take the signet ring of her husband, and therewith affix the royal seal that the document might go forth with authority. Apparently, Ahab asked no question about the means which his wife meant to employ."[3]

CREATING SOUL TIES WITH PRAYER WARRIORS

Jezebel tries to create soul ties with people in the group. Jezebel had a serious soul tie with Ahab, and as a result, he became her puppet.

The Bible doesn't use the phrase "soul tie" but it is a biblical concept. A soul tie is a deep emotional bond between two people.

Prophesying, Teaching, Undermining, and Dominating

There are healthy soul ties and toxic soul ties. Divine soul ties and demonic soul ties. There are at least four ways you develop soul ties.

A soul tie happens when people's souls are knit together in close relationships, like in the case of Jonathan and David. We read about this special connection in 1 Samuel 18:1 (NKJV), "Now when he had finished speaking to Saul, the soul of Jonathan was knit to the soul of David, and Jonathan loved him as his own soul." I've had soul ties with friends that wound up being massively toxic. You probably have too.

A soul tie can form when you make vows to or covenants with someone. Numbers 30:2 (NKJV) tells us, "If a man makes a vow to the Lord, or swears an oath to bind himself by some agreement, he shall not break his word; he shall do according to all that proceeds out of his mouth."

Much the same, sharing personal information in confidence with a friend can create a soul tie, as can pledging a vow of loyalty to them. Be careful not to enter a covenant relationship too quickly. Soul ties may start off healthy within the family unit or with friends, but they become unhealthy when sin or evil spirits are involved.

You can even unknowingly make vows with spirits by saying things like, "I'll never let anyone hurt me like that again" or "I will always protect my back from now on." In fact, when you say such words, the spirit of Jezebel (and other spirits) hears you and sees it as an invitation to provide perverted protection by coming to your defense when you face unfair treatment. I shared my story earlier in this book.

When you feel wronged, you may tend to manifest self-preserving behavior that's literally influenced by God's spiritual enemies.

This is sinful in many ways, but mostly because we are supposed to trust in the Lord with all our hearts—not lean to our own understanding or lean on a demon power to protect us.

If you have a soul tie with someone operating in a Jezebel or Ahab spirit, it is difficult to resist their influence in your life. You have to break the soul tie. I always say, "You have to break the Jezebel alignment before you can break the Jezebel assignment."

SINISTER CHARACTER ASSASSINATION

Jezebel is a character assassin. Jezebelic intercessors tell others things about people that are not true. We see this plainly in Queen Jezebel's dastardly maneuvers against Naboth, who possessed a field that Ahab coveted. We read the account in 1 Kings 21:1-16 (NKJV):

> *And it came to pass after these things that Naboth the Jezreelite had a vineyard which was in Jezreel, next to the palace of Ahab king of Samaria. So Ahab spoke to Naboth, saying, "Give me your vineyard, that I may have it for a vegetable garden, because it is near, next to my house; and for it I will give you a vineyard better than it. Or, if it seems good to you, I will give you its worth in money."*
>
> *But Naboth said to Ahab, "The Lord forbid that I should give the inheritance of my fathers to you!"*
>
> *So Ahab went into his house sullen and displeased because of the word which Naboth the Jezreelite had spoken to him; for he had said, "I will not give you the*

inheritance of my fathers." And he lay down on his bed, and turned away his face, and would eat no food. But Jezebel his wife came to him, and said to him, "Why is your spirit so sullen that you eat no food?"

He said to her, "Because I spoke to Naboth the Jezreelite, and said to him, 'Give me your vineyard for money; or else, if it pleases you, I will give you another vineyard for it.' And he answered, 'I will not give you my vineyard.'"

Then Jezebel his wife said to him, "You now exercise authority over Israel! Arise, eat food, and let your heart be cheerful; I will give you the vineyard of Naboth the Jezreelite." And she wrote letters in Ahab's name, sealed them with his seal, and sent the letters to the elders and the nobles who were dwelling in the city with Naboth. She wrote in the letters, saying,

Proclaim a fast, and seat Naboth with high honor among the people; and seat two men, scoundrels, before him to bear witness against him, saying, "You have blasphemed God and the king." Then take him out, and stone him, that he may die.

So the men of his city, the elders and nobles who were inhabitants of his city, did as Jezebel had sent to them, as it was written in the letters which she had sent to them. They proclaimed a fast, and seated Naboth with high honor among the people. And two men, scoundrels, came in and sat before him; and the scoundrels witnessed against him, against Naboth, in the presence of the people, saying, "Naboth has blasphemed God and the king!" Then they took him outside the city and

> *stoned him with stones, so that he died. Then they sent to Jezebel, saying, "Naboth has been stoned and is dead."*
>
> *And it came to pass, when Jezebel heard that Naboth had been stoned and was dead, that Jezebel said to Ahab, "Arise, take possession of the vineyard of Naboth the Jezreelite, which he refused to give you for money; for Naboth is not alive, but dead." So it was, when Ahab heard that Naboth was dead, that Ahab got up and went down to take possession of the vineyard of Naboth the Jezreelite.*

Jezebel discredited Naboth and let others do the dirty work of stoning him. She planted a seed, but the blood wasn't literally on her hands. This is how high-level Jezebelic intercessors work.

OFFENSIVE AND EASILY OFFENDED

Jezebel is offensive and easily offended by righteousness. Jezebel is offended when she doesn't get what she wants. *Easton's Bible Dictionary* reads, "Jezebel, Ahab's wife, was grievously offended at Naboth's refusal to part with his vineyard. By a crafty and cruel plot she compassed his death."[4]

If you want to see Jezebel's intercessor manifest, just say the word "no" and refuse to be moved off that stance with demonic reasoning, threats and intimidation, or even crocodile tears.

Someone who is easily offended is quick to argue and defend themselves. They are also quick to anger and dispute the scriptural admonition to be slow to anger (see James 1:9). Jezebel's intercessors get their feelings hurt easily because they are already hurt and wounded. Jezebel's intercessors keep playing comments or actions over and over in their minds and growing resentful.

JEALOUS AND COMPETITIVE

Jezebel is competitive because she wants to be seen and admired. She doesn't like when others have the spotlight. We don't compete in prayer meetings; we cooperate. It's not a competition. It's a cooperation with the Spirit of God to see His will come to pass in the earth. But Jezebel's intercessors can't help themselves. Their prayers are meant to one-up the last prayer warrior.

Paul knew competition would be an issue in the Body of Christ, which is why he wrote, "Let nothing be done through selfish ambition or conceit, but in lowliness of mind let each esteem others better than himself" (Phil. 2:3 NKJV). Paul told the carnal Corinthian church: "Whether therefore ye eat, or drink, or whatsoever ye do, do all to the glory of God" (1 Cor. 10:31 KJV). If eating and drinking should be to the glory of God, how much more so prayer and intercession?

The preacher warned in Ecclesiastes 4:4 (NLT), "Then I observed that most people are motivated to success because they envy their neighbors. But this, too, is meaningless—like chasing the wind." Jezebel's intercessors are not effective in their intercession because they are chasing the wind—chasing promotion, chasing visibility, and chasing idols. Beware Jezebel's intercessors.

PRAYER

Father, in the name of Jesus, thank You for sharpening my prophetic edge and discernment so I can be a guardian of prayer. Thank You for teaching me to spot Jezebel's intercessors by the spirit and not just by natural maneuvers. Teach me to separate the principality from the personality so I can walk in love with the person but stand against the devil's devices to disrupt prayer.

NOTES

1. Charles John Ellicott, Rev. C.J. Ball, *Elliot's Commentary*, s.v. 1 Kings 21:8, (London, 1905) https://biblehub.com/commentaries/1_kings/21-8.htm.

2. Robert Jamieson, A.R. Fausset, and David Brown, *Jameison-Fausset-Brown Bible Commentary*, s.v. 1 Kings 21:8, (1882), ibid.

3. J.R. Lumby, *Cambridge Bible for Schools and Colleges*, s.v. 1 Kings 21:8, (Cambridge University Press, 1886), ibid.

4. Matthew George Easton, *Easton's Bible Dictionary*, s.v. "Naboth," (1893), https://biblehub.com/topical/n/naboth.htm.

CHAPTER 8

GROOMING SONS, SPIES, MESSENGERS, AND FALSE
PROPHETS

Jacob looked like the ideal candidate for our worship director position at Awakening House of Prayer. He was seasoned, skilled, and carried a breaker anointing. You might say that we could "tick all the boxes" as the ideal man for the job.

There was only one problem: His wife had a Jezebel spirit. Red flags were raised when Jacob told us his wife had a prophetic word for us, started to share it, then pulled back under the guise of "not wanting to misrepresent the word." He urged me to speak with his wife and insisted she was a brilliant intercessor. But his wife was never available.

They were stringing me along with the hope of some life-changing prophecy in true Jezebelic splendor. Thankfully, this was not my first rodeo in the realm of spiritual warfare and it didn't move me. I never asked about it again and they never brought it up.

Without any conversation with us, Jacob's wife drove the hiring process from that point on—and started making unreasonable demands. While we were just looking to hire Jacob for worship, she was essentially pressing to be our head intercessor. She wanted a chief position in the ministry where she would carry influence and authority. And her going rate was far beyond our budget.

When we kindly suggested we were looking to hire only one person, we were chastised. Jacob's name was on the e-mail but it was clearly not Jacob's hand behind the words on the screen, which were laced with witchcraft. It was reminiscent of how Queen Jezebel took Ahab's signet ring, usurping his authority to forward her agenda (see 1 Kings 21:8).

Discerning the spirit behind the promise of prophecy and demand to be our heavily paid intercessory prayer leader, we immediately ended all negotiations and thanked God for helping us escape Jezebel's snare. Not everything that glitters is gold. Sometimes, Jezebel is hiding behind the glitter. Unfortunately, the attack rippled as they continued to charge our credit card repeatedly for months for what was supposed to be a one-time reimbursement of flights—and when contacted they refused to refund the money.

As I said in the previous chapters, we need to discern Jezebel's intercessors in our lives, businesses, and ministries, or they will wreak havoc on the prayer ministry like Jacob's wife did. Jezebel, like any other spirit, works to steal, kill, and destroy. Jezebel does this mainly through seduction. But if Jezebel can't seduce you, she will work to overthrow you, your family, your business, your ministry, or whatever she can infiltrate.

I pointed out a few ways to spot Jezebel's intercessors in action in the last chapter. We'll wrap up our study on discerning Jezebel in the pages ahead. I know I've said this a few times before, but it bears repeating: These points are not intended to be a checklist, but a picture of the diverse ways in which Jezebel's intercessors may operate.

What's more, just because someone behaves poorly in a prayer meeting doesn't necessarily make them one of Jezebel's intercessors. They could be operating in the flesh or the soul or some other spirit. Likewise, one doesn't have to manifest all these behaviors to be operating in a Jezebel spirit. We must rely on the Holy Spirit's discernment and wisdom that comes from experience.

BIRTHING SPIRITUAL SONS AND DAUGHTERS

We talked about eunuchs in the last chapter, but all of Jezebel's followers aren't eunuchs. Some have greater proximity. We call those spiritual sons and daughters. Consider again Revelation 2:20-23 (NLT):

> *But I have this complaint against you. You are permitting that woman—that Jezebel who calls herself a prophet—to lead my servants astray. She teaches them to commit sexual sin and to eat food offered to idols. I gave her time to repent, but she does not want to turn away from her immorality.*
>
> *Therefore, I will throw her on a bed of suffering, and those who commit adultery with her will suffer greatly unless they repent and turn away from her evil deeds. I will strike her children dead.*

Read that again, "I will strike her children dead." The New King James Version says, "I will kill her children with death." The New American Standard Bible says, "And I will kill her children with plague." The Amplified Bible denotes that her children are her "followers" and they will be thoroughly annihilated. Jezebel has spiritual sons and daughters. She pollutes them. She perverts them. And she sets them on a broad path that leads to destruction.

Why does Jezebel want spiritual children? She wants to train them in her ways so they can help build her kingdom and propagate her deception and spread her seduction like a virus. Jezebel knows her children will defend her against false accusations, so she works to control their minds and hearts to fulfill her desires by dangling rewards in their face. Jezebel works to woo them away from their first love and subtly take the place of Jesus in their lives.

Although Jesus was talking to scribes and Pharisees in Matthew 23:15 (NKJV), the woe He pronounces in this verse could just as easily apply to Jezebel: "Woe to you, scribes and Pharisees, hypocrites! For you travel land and sea to win one proselyte, and when he is won, you make him twice as much a son of hell as yourselves." Jezebel's spiritual children become a brood of vipers.

DEPLOYING SPIES

Jezebel's intercessors infiltrate any group they join and become information-seeking spies. They aren't satisfied with what the Holy Spirit wants to show them about a person, place, or thing. They want to use their demonic shovel to dig around in things that aren't their business. You might say they "pry to prey."

Jezebel's intercessors want information because information is power. They can use the information about the pastor, the church, or another prayer warrior as they strategically plan who to target and how to manipulate and seduce them.

We've had more than one person come to Awakening House of Prayer and ask inappropriate questions about me. Make no mistake: Jezebel's intercessors may start out with simple and seemingly harmless questions, but inappropriate questions will soon follow. She targets those who seem closest to her next victim.

Jezebelic intercessors scout out social media, looking for personal information about what someone is going through or dealing with so she can provide false prophetic comfort to people in their time of need. Don't air your personal laundry on Facebook. Jezebel will see it and offer to help you clean it up, but she'll only make it worse. Yes, she'll position herself as a concerned listening ear, but she is really gathering information to use against you later. Alternatively, Jezebel's intercessors gather information so they can prophesy to people words that never came from the Lord.

Jezebel's intercessors eavesdrop on conversations. We had a Jezebelic intercessor in our ministry who was always within earshot. She positioned herself purposely far enough away not to seem obtrusive, but close enough to hear. She'd do this under the guise of sweeping or dusting. Jezebel's intercessors don't mind violating your privacy.

Paul dealt with spies and eavesdroppers. He spoke of them in Galatians 2:4 (NKJV), "And this occurred because of false brethren secretly brought in (who came in by stealth to spy out our liberty which we have in Christ Jesus, that they might bring us into bondage)." Jezebel's intercessors want to determine what your weaknesses are, or the weakness of those with whom you are working, so she can bring you into bondage to her will.

DISPATCHING MESSENGERS

Jezebel's intercessors use eunuchs and spiritual sons and daughters—as well as unsuspecting believers—as messengers. It may have been a eunuch who delivered the fearful curse to Elijah that sent him running into the wilderness hoping to die after defeating the false prophets at Mount Carmel. We see this in 1 Kings 19:1-3 (NKJV):

> *And Ahab told Jezebel all that Elijah had done, also how he had executed all the prophets with the sword. Then Jezebel sent a messenger to Elijah, saying, "So let the gods do to me, and more also, if I do not make your life as the life of one of them by tomorrow about this time." And when he saw that, he arose and ran for his life, and went to Beersheba, which belongs to Judah, and left his servant there.*

Jezebel doesn't do her own dirty work most of the time. She sends other people to do it for her. She thinks her hands are clean, but as the mastermind behind the attack, the Lord will hold her accountable for the messes she makes in lives, ministries, and businesses.

STRONG INTIMIDATION AND SPIRITUAL ABUSE

Jezebel operates in intimidation and spiritual abuse. She uses intimidation as a tool, just like control and manipulation. In fact, she uses intimidation to control and manipulate. The intimidation usually comes in the form of threats.

Jezebel demands blind submission, and when she doesn't get it, she goes on a warpath against the one who rebels against her illegitimate authority. Many people who endure spiritual abuse don't see the depths of the impact until they escape from Jezebel's clutches.

I had never heard the words "spiritual abuse" until I escaped a controlling Jezebelic ministry where the subtle practice ran rampant. Someone close to me who had observed the behavior in the church I attended recommended a book called *The Subtle Power of Spiritual Abuse*. The book answered a lot of questions for me and I would highly suggest you read it if you have encountered spiritual abuse in your journey.

What exactly is spiritual abuse? Jeff VanVonderen, co-author of the classic book *The Subtle Power of Spiritual Abuse*, explains it this way: "Spiritual abuse occurs when someone in a position of spiritual authority…misuses that authority placing themselves over God's people to control, coerce or manipulate them for seemingly godly purposes which are really their own."[1]

Spiritual abuse is hardly a new phenomenon. You can find instances in the Bible of spiritual leaders exploiting people to build their kingdoms. In Jeremiah 8:11 (NIV) the Lord called out the abuse of prophets and priests, saying, "They dress the wound of my people as though it were not serious."

Among other telltale signs in the book, Johnson and VanVonderen explain that in toxic systems it is more important to act according to the word of a leader who has "a word" for you than to act according to what you know to be true from Scripture or simply from your spiritual growth history.

Jezebel is in competition with Jesus to build her cultish kingdom. She wounds believers in order to control them, but the gates of hell will not prevail against the church.

SEDUCTIVE FALSE PROPHETS

Jezebel's intercessors love to prophesy. The truth is prophetic words don't carry the same weight as Scripture, and you can hear from God for yourself. When you rely on other people to tell you what God is saying, you open the door to control and manipulation.

Remember, Jesus said Jezebel called herself a prophetess (see Rev. 2:20). Often—not always, but often—Jezebel's intercessors will consider themselves prophets or even apostles. Like the Jezebel in the church at Thyatira, they are self-appointed and self-anointed. They may very well be prophetic, but they are tapping into a familiar spirit. They are deceived.

Why do Jezebel's intercessors position themselves as prophets? Because it gives them more credibility when they prophesy. The office of the prophet carries a prophetic authority that many believers, especially if they are not discerning, find hard to defy. They put more weight on words that come from a prophet than an everyday intercessor.

I was reading an article in Salon.com. It caused my jaw to drop. Here's the text:

> On the day I realized I was a prophet, I left my home in Colorado and began to hitch-hike to the U.N. I needed to save the world from its various evils. And I needed to go—now.
>
> I spent the next several days wandering around the northeast, trying to decipher messages. I found codes in places where codes didn't exist. I finally found my way back home, thanks to a quiet and generous woman who lived somewhere in rural Massachusetts, and when I got back, I explained to my parents that I was on a mission and this was God's will. I'm sure there was some stuff about aliens and conspiracies in there, too.
>
> And so, a week after my adventure began, I woke up in the psych ward of Boulder Community Hospital, and I spent the next seven days condemned to a hospital bed with waterproof sheets in a ward with eight other people who either didn't talk or rambled so incoherently that it was impossible to understand them.[2]

It turns out, he wasn't prophetic at all. He was schizophrenic. Jezebel's intercessors may not be schizophrenic, but the Jezebel spirit may convince them they are apostles or prophets. And they really believe it. Maybe someone else operating in a Jezebel spirit prophesied them into the office in a prayer line. Either way, it's a dangerous deception to speak what some other spirit is saying and attribute it to the Lord.

I can't tell you how many people come to my church or contact me through other means and the first thing they want me to know is that they are a prophet. That always causes me to take a beat. Their identity is in a gift, perhaps even a gift they don't have, and they want everyone to know about it because it makes them feel special.

This is the sign of someone deceived by pride, which is often rooted in insecurities. Jezebel loves to manipulate people through their insecurities. Remember, pride often compensates for rejection. Paul offered these wise Spirit-inspired words in Romans 12:3 (NKJV): "For I say, through the grace given to me, to everyone who is among you, not to think of himself more highly than he ought to think, but to think soberly, as God has dealt to each one a measure of faith."

JEZEBEL COVETS PLATFORM

Jezebel's intercessors want to use your platform—or someone else's platform—to build her own platform. She wants a place to perform. I mentioned this in passing in an earlier chapter but I want to zero in on it.

The Old Testament Jezebel used Ahab's kingdom to build her own demonic kingdom. The Book of Revelation Jezebel used the pastor's platform to launch her own teaching ministry.

I can't tell you how many people with Jezebelic agendas have tried to cozy up to me to get on my platform. There was the young prophet who jumped from covering to covering, tapping into new audiences along the way. There was the businessman-turned-prophet who copied everything I did and skimmed off the top of my following to build his own ministry.

And I'll always remember an email I received from someone thanking me in advance for promoting them on my platform in an hour-long interview about their new book. They didn't ask if I would like to do an interview and wait for an answer. No, they presumptuously thanked me in advance for taking the time and gave me several dates and times to choose from. When I didn't comply with their manipulative e-mail, they started slandering me.

A young man who was hurt at a megachurch started coming to AHOP some years ago. He had leadership potential, but he was hurt and bitter. He was constantly pushing me to give him a position and let him pray for people at the altar. I didn't even know him. That was troublesome, as well as how he called the Holy Spirit an *it*. "He said, I have the Holy Spirit I want to use it." The Holy Spirit is not an it. When I told the young man "not yet," he left.

CURSES AND JUDGMENT

High-level Jezebelic intercessors may actually curse people who get in their way. After Elijah slew all the false prophets at Mount Carmel, Ahab went back and told Jezebel what happened. She should have repented then. Instead, she released a curse against Elijah:

> *So Jezebel sent this message to Elijah: "May the gods strike me and even kill me if by this time tomorrow I*

have not killed you just as you killed them" (1 Kings 19:2 NLT).

This was more than a threat; it was a death curse. The death curse released witchcraft at Elijah, who sat under a tree wishing he was dead. The curse didn't ultimately succeed, but it did derail Elijah for a season.

As I was wrapping up the writing of this book, I experienced this personally. There was a man who joined Awakening Prayer Hubs. He seemed like an odd bird, but we don't judge by appearances. He came to our Intercessor's Invitational, which begins with the Friday night prayer room. The prayer room was packed, yet he tried to make his way to the front row to give me a gift. Someone thanked him and intercepted it. He left.

Clearly offended, he sent a scathing letter that was several pages long and too long to include, but it sounded like this:

> My Troubling Noticings [sic]; which I'm having to interceed [sic] during my email due to the spirit of confusion which has come through from your ministry…I want to include a troublesome experience that I believe will point out to the ministry a spiritual attack that you all are under which should be evident by the way that this email is clear and not being understood and I am also someone a part of your Seer Company is noticing…. All of this will be important later as it stands for 3 things; perversion; confusion; and witchcraft.

He went on to threaten us, curse the ministry, and try to intimidate us by saying he was emailing our supporters these and other accusations and more. The gift he left was a box that smelled like death. It literally smelled like a dead animal was inside. The box was filled with dirty socks, wine, strange photographs, half-burnt candles, and other items that seemed associated with witchcraft. My staff had to put on gloves just to go through the box and dispose of the items. Remember, Jezebel can work through men.

PRAYER

Father, in the name of Jesus, help me to discern the operations of Jezebel in any way, shape, or form that it manifests. Help me not to merely tick down boxes, but to lean into Your heart and hear Your voice warning me of the assignment. Help me not to miss Jezebel's intercessors hiding behind masks I haven't seen before or working in ways that I haven't known before.

NOTES

1. David Johnson and Jeff VanVonderen, *The Subtle Power of Spiritual Abuse* (Bloomington, MN: Bethany House, 1991), 45.

2. Michael Hedrick, "I Thought I Was A Prophet," Salon, August 2, 2013, https://www.salon.com/2013/08/02/i_thought_i_was_a_prophet.

CHAPTER 9

AVOIDING TAPPING INTO WITCHCRAFT
PRAYERS

We were praying for Ukraine during the nation's battle to preserve its national sovereignty. Fervent, compassionate intercession was going forth and we were touching the heart of God.

God's presence was strong. Our intercessors were determined to stand and withstand until Russia withdrew its troops—and committed to interceding for the Russian people who never asked for the war.

Suddenly, one of Jezebel's intercessors took the mic. Keep in mind that, more than once, we had instructed the gatekeeper not to allow this woman to pray openly because she was too hurt and wounded—and those hurts and wounds peppered her prayer. We were laboring to get her healed and whole but knew from past experience with her that her public intercession often opposed God's will and released witchcraft into the atmosphere.

We were hit with a double whammy. The prayer leader who was charged with guarding the mic had some unknown common ground with Jezebel. The spirit influencing her caused her to defy our instructions and hand over the mic. As it turns out, both these women were operating in the Jezebel spirit—and Jezebel used them to throw a coup in the prayer room. It wasn't premeditated by the demon influencing them. What happened next was disastrous.

Jezebel's intercessor took the mic and proceeded to levy heavy curses against Russia and the Russian people. She began to call for famine in the land, for the water to dry up, and for other ills and woes to come into the nation of Russia. Of course, this was offensive on many levels and not the heart of God. Some got up and walked out, thinking our leadership was in agreement with these witchcraft prayers. Our drummer at the time, who is Russian, got so offended with the church and with the prophetic movement that he left and never came back.

Now, this is an extreme example of witchcraft prayers, complete with overt doom, gloom, and curses. But make no mistake: Any Christian can tap into witchcraft prayers, and perhaps not in the way you think. I'm not talking only about releasing word curses, incantations, spells, and potions. Witches are not the only ones who release witchcraft prayers. A Christian who is praying to God in the name of Jesus can release a witchcraft prayer without knowing it. It's subtle, but the discerning can hear the spirit behind witchcraft prayers.

UNDERSTANDING WITCHCRAFT PRAYER

So what is a witchcraft prayer? Witchcraft prayers can be hexes, vexes, incantations, and spells. Witchcraft prayers can be curses. Witchcraft prayers can intend to bring people great harm, including harm to their minds, families, finances, businesses, ministries, health, and more. Witchcraft prayers can invite the enemy to wreak havoc on the life of an innocent soul.

Most Christians—even Jezebel's intercessors—aren't praying straight-up witchcraft in the sense we imagine when we first hear this dark word. No, in the Christian world witchcraft prayers often sound more benign. But make no mistake, the power of death can still be released into an atmosphere, a person's life, a city, a nation, or a circumstance through witchcraft prayers, even if they sound innocent enough.

The challenge for many is discerning witchcraft prayers from the mouths of Christians, especially when the person isn't intentionally trying to do any harm. Indeed, it can be difficult for the undiscerning to recognize witchcraft prayers because these petitions often come from a sincere heart. These supplications are often sincere and offered with great passion. The person praying may not even know they are praying witchcraft prayers! Remember that. We're not wrestling against flesh and blood, but principalities and powers (see Eph. 6:12).

JEZEBEL'S WITCHCRAFT PRAYERS

So the question is, what is a witchcraft prayer in the context of Jezebel's intercessors? Simply put, a witchcraft prayer is when you pray your own will instead of God's will. Witchcraft prayers are not Spirit-led but flesh-led. They are not God-inspired but soul-inspired. You could call these utterances carnal prayers, but I call them witchcraft prayers because that's what this type of intercession is releasing.

Sometimes Jezebel's intercessors *do* know what they are doing. Other times they do not. But because they are defiled, Jezebel's intercessors are often used as puppets to pray against God's will or lead others to pray outside His will, which never leads to anything good. At best, the time spent in intercession is wasted. At worst, witchcraft prayer gives the enemy an open door to attack.

Jezebel's witchcraft prayers aim to control people and situations. Rather than trusting God to bring His will to pass, the Jezebelic intercessor asserts his or her will into the mix. Even if you are praying for God's will, you can't tell God how to do His job. Like tumors, some witchcraft prayers are benign. They are soulish prayers that fall to the ground. God does not hear them. Others are malignant and work to steal, kill, and destroy (see John 10:10). Either way, we don't want to join with, agree to, or tolerate witchcraft prayers—ever.

A benign witchcraft prayer might sound like this: "God, cause my prodigal to come home now!" God is not going to make anyone do anything. He doesn't violate our will, so He's not going to answer prayers asking Him to violate someone's will. The prodigal son in the Bible came home when he got to the end of himself. Instead, we might pray for God to encourage the prodigal with His love.

Another example is self-focused witchcraft prayers, which may sound like this, "God, speak to the pastor about putting me on the worship team." That's a self-centered prayer. It assumes the pastor doesn't pray or doesn't hear from God. It assumes that God wants you on the worship team, when He may not. Instead, we should pray, "God, if it's Your will, would You open a door for me on the worship team?" That's the prayer of consecration.

Another example is, "God, make my husband stop acting that way." Instead, our prayer should be, "God, help me to walk in love with my husband while You are working in him to form Christ's character in Him." Now, do you get the idea? Essentially, in a witchcraft prayer you are saying, "God, give me what I want." That may or may not be in your best interests. It may or may not be God's will. It may flat-out oppose God's will.

A friend of mine who is not saved was having a lot of trouble with his ex-wife. He asked me to pray for him. He said, "Pray I don't choke her and that if I do choke her, I choke some sense into her." Of course, I didn't pray that because it's a negative prayer. Nothing good can come of that, and it's still agreeing that he might choke her. Instead, I prayed that God would give him His peace and self-control.

There are more malignant examples of witchcraft prayers that proceed from the mouth of Jezebel's intercessors, though. Examples might be, "Lord, remove that person from his position on the worship team and put me in my rightful place." Or, "Lord, bring my competition low and cause my business to prosper." Or, "Lord, make that person my spouse." These types of prayers can release clouds of confusion over people or even open a door for the enemy to work in their life.

One of the dangers of Jezebel's intercessors is that they don't always release witchcraft prayers in a public setting like the woman in our prayer room. You may never hear the prayer, so you can't bind it before it has a chance to wreak havoc. Often, Jezebel's intercessors pray flowery and eloquent prayers in public, but fleshly, carnal, witchcraft prayers when no one is listening. Only later do you see the effects of Jezebel's intercession.

WICKED WORKS OF WITCHCRAFT

Jezebel's witchcraft prayers often fall into the Galatians 5 category of works of the flesh. In Galatians 5:19-21 (NKJV), Paul the apostle writes:

> *Now the works of the flesh are evident, which are: adultery, fornication, uncleanness, lewdness, idolatry, sorcery, hatred, contentions, jealousies, outbursts of wrath, selfish ambitions, dissensions, heresies, envy, murders, drunkenness, revelries, and the like.*

Many believers feel good about themselves when they read Paul's list because they aren't participating in these activities. They spend more time in the prayer closet than they do in front of the TV. But that doesn't mean we're not praying witchcraft prayers. We need to look at these tendencies in us before we go on a witch hunt. We need, too, to understand what prayer really is and the laws of prayer so we don't violate them. I talk more about this in my book *The Intercessor's Devotional*.

Galatians 5:20 speaks of the work of the flesh as witchcraft. Different translations use different words, such as sorcery. If you look at the Greek word for witchcraft in this verse, it is used as a metaphor for idolatry. And obviously anything we do out of the flesh is rebellion. Another way to put it is, rebellion is rooted in the flesh.

JEZEBEL'S REBELLIOUS PRAYERS

Because Jezebel hates God, this demon will lead intercessors to pray rebellious prayers. Consider the words of Paul the apostle in Romans 8:7 (AMPC), "[That is] because the mind of the flesh [with its carnal thoughts and purposes] is hostile to God, for it does not submit itself to God's Law; indeed it cannot." When Jezebel works to renew the mind of the intercessor, the intercessor doesn't know that their prayers have become hostile to God. They are deceived and sincerely don't see it.

Paul also offered this wisdom in Galatians 5:17 (AMPC):

> *For the desires of the flesh are opposed to the [Holy] Spirit, and the [desires of the] Spirit are opposed to the flesh (godless human nature); for these are antagonistic to each other [continually withstanding and in conflict with each other], so that you are not free but are prevented from doing what you desire to do.*

Because Jezebel's intercessors are often influenced by a spirit other than the Spirit of God, these prayers are antagonistic and in conflict with what the Spirit of God desires.

God is clear—rebellion is as the sin of witchcraft. He says so in 1 Samuel 15:23 (NKJV), "For rebellion is as the sin of witchcraft, and stubbornness is as iniquity and idolatry. Because you have rejected the word of the Lord, He also has rejected you from being king." The New International Version puts it this way, "For rebellion is like the sin of divination, and arrogance like the evil of idolatry." The English Standard Version says, "For rebellion is as the sin of divination, and presumption is as iniquity and idolatry."

The New American Standard Bible offers, "For rebellion is as the sin of divination, and insubordination is as iniquity and idolatry." The Christian Standard Bible says, "For rebellion is like the sin of divination, and defiance is like wickedness and idolatry." And *The Message* brings it home: "Not doing what God tells you is far worse than fooling around in the occult. Getting self-important around God is far worse than making deals with your dead ancestors."

We all have flesh, and any of us can come under the influence of a Jezebel spirit in our prayers. We need to avoid rebellious, idolatrous prayers. Paul said in Romans 7:18 (AMPC), "For I know that nothing good dwells within me, that is, in my flesh." We need to crucify our flesh so that we don't pray from our carnal nature. We need to submit ourselves to God before we submit our prayers to God. We need to die to self and present ourselves as living sacrifices unto God (see Rom. 12:1). When we do, Jezebel won't have any room to infiltrate our prayers.

THE DANGER OF WITCHCRAFT PRAYERS

Demons counterfeit the operations of angels. So when we pray witchcraft prayers, the demons come to execute those words. Witchcraft prayers unleash demon powers that tempt and seduce people to think and do what we want them to think and do. The targets of witchcraft prayers may come under something like a spell and begin to act in ways that oppose their true desires—and God's desires for them.

Jesus said in Matthew 12:37 (NKJV), "For by your words you will be justified, and by your words you will be condemned." The word *condemn* in that verse means to make a judgment against. In the realm of witchcraft prayers, your words are either seeking justice or inviting the enemy's condemnation in someone's life. Also consider Christ's words in Luke 6:45 (NKJV):

> *A good man out of the good treasure of his heart brings forth good; and an evil man out of the evil treasure of his heart brings forth evil. For out of the abundance of the heart his mouth speaks.*

We know that whatever is not of faith is sin (see Rom. 14:23). Witchcraft prayers are sin. You aren't praying from a heart posture of faith. You are praying with a heart posture of control. My great-grandmother was at her wits' end with one of her sons. After he came back from World War II, he acquired a terrible drinking habit. It was probably because of Post-Traumatic Stress Disorder (PTSD). Back then, of course, people didn't know anything about PTSD.

My grandmother didn't want him to die a drunkard. She was a godly woman and feared he would get in a brawl or harm himself. So she prayed, "Lord, do whatever it takes to keep him from bringing that bottle to his mouth again." Well, she meant well, but the devil is legalistic. The next day, her son shot his arm off and walked around with one arm for the rest of his life. But that didn't stop him from drinking.

GOD STRICTLY FORBIDS WITCHCRAFT IN ALL FORMS

God forbids witchcraft, even witchcraft released in ignorance. Scripture warns us not be ignorant of the devil's devices (see 2 Cor. 2:11). We can't claim ignorance. We need to rightly divide the word of truth. Deuteronomy 18:9-14 (NKJV) offers a strong warning against witchcraft:

> *When you come into the land which the Lord your God is giving you, you shall not learn to follow the abominations of those nations. There shall not be found among you anyone who makes his son or his daughter pass through the fire, or one who practices witchcraft, or a soothsayer, or one who interprets omens, or a sorcerer, or one who conjures spells, or a medium, or a spiritist, or one who calls up the dead.*
>
> *For all who do these things are an abomination to the Lord, and because of these abominations the Lord your God drives them out from before you. You shall be blameless before the Lord your God. For these nations*

which you will dispossess listened to soothsayers and diviners; but as for you, the Lord your God has not appointed such for you.

You are not an abomination to Him, but witchcraft prayers are. Heaven will not be filled with witches, adulterers, haters, and fornicators. That's why we need to repent. Inspired by the Holy Spirit, Paul said those who, among other works of the flesh, practice witchcraft will not inherit the Kingdom of God (see Gal. 5:21).

Matthew Henry's Commentary puts it this way: "The works of the flesh are many and manifest. And these sins will shut men out of heaven. Yet what numbers, calling themselves Christians, live in these, and say they hope for heaven!"[1] *Matthew Poole's Commentary* offers: "That they which do such things shall not inherit the kingdom of God; that they who ordinarily do these things, and do not only live in such practices, but die without repentance for them, shall never be saved."[2]

Of course, I'm not saying you will go to hell for praying witchcraft prayers, especially in ignorance. But it grieves the Holy Spirit we're trying to please.

YOUR WILL BE DONE

We can avoid witchcraft prayers by knowing the will of the Lord and not inserting our will into the mix. When Jesus' disciples asked for a lesson in prayer, He recited to them The Lord's Prayer. The prayer in Matthew 6 starts this way, "Our Father in heaven, hallowed be

Your name. Your kingdom come. Your will be done on earth as it is in heaven" (Matt. 6:9-10 NKJV).

The Greek word for *will* in that verse is *thelema*. According to *The KJV New Testament Greek Lexicon* it means, "what one wishes or has determined shall be done, of the purpose of God to bless mankind through Christ, commands, precepts, will, choice, inclination, desire, pleasure."

When we pray, we are supposed to be praying for God's will to be done, for His purposes to be accomplished, for His choices, inclinations, desires, and pleasures to come to pass. When we pray, we are supposed to be coming into agreement with what God wants so that He can bring an answer that helps people and advances His Kingdom.

Again, when we pray our will instead of God's will, it's witchcraft—even if we aren't trying to pray wrongly. Sometimes witchcraft prayers are released in innocence and immaturity and cause no real harm. But when the motives of mankind are wrong, we find ourselves in more dangerous territory. Jezebel hates the voice of God. She hates the Spirit of God. She hates you and she hates those for whom you are praying.

CHECKING HEART MOTIVES

We can avoid witchcraft prayers by keeping our hands clean and our hearts pure (see Ps. 24:4-5). Ultimately, it's the motive that matters. Your motive should be love. In other words, love should influence your intercession, not self-will, which can spawn control, manipulation, intimidation, and ultimately charismatic witchcraft.

Witchcraft prayers can also emanate out of fear and anxiety. If your prayer is not rooted in the will of God or seeking the will of God, or if your prayer asks God to make someone do something instead of helping someone do something, it's in the realm of witchcraft. That's because your motive is not submitted to God—it's submitted to your own desires or even devilish desires.

Remember, we may think we know what is best for someone, but we have to pray for God's will to be done. God knows best. We know God's will in many situations because God's Word is His will. But sometimes it's not that easy, especially when our emotions, our money, or our time are involved.

Keep in mind the words of James, the apostle of practical faith. He offers one reason why people tap into witchcraft prayers:

> *You lust and do not have. You murder and covet and cannot obtain. You fight and war. Yet you do not have because you do not ask. You ask and do not receive, because you ask amiss, that you may spend it on your pleasures* (James 4:2-3 NKJV).

By contrast, look at the words of John the Beloved in 1 John 5:14-15 (NKJV):

> *Now this is the confidence that we have in Him, that if we ask anything according to His will, He hears us. And if we know that He hears us, whatever we ask, we know that we have the petitions that we have asked of Him.*

So you could say, if we ask anything that is not agreeable to His will, He will not entertain that prayer. But the devil might. Keep in mind, angels and demons both come for your words. After Daniel prayed, an angel told him, "I have come because of your words" (Daniel 10:12 NKJV). And in Psalm 103:20, "Bless the Lord, all ye his angels: you that are mighty in strength, and execute his word, hearkening to the voice of his orders" (Douay-Rheims Bible). The enemy also comes for your words—including your prayers.

SIGNS YOU ARE THE VICTIM OF WITCHCRAFT PRAYERS

There are signs you are under a charismatic witchcraft attack. Confusion is a primary sign. Confusion is part of the curse of the law (see Deut. 28:28). God is not the author of confusion (see 1 Cor. 4:33). If you are confused as to whether something is of God, that may be the first sign it's not. A charismatic witchcraft spell works on your identity—or I should say works against your identity. You become dependent on the leader rather than God to make decisions.

Advanced charismatic witchcraft prayers and spells work to create soul ties between you and the wicked intercessor so you will feel connected with them and their ministry. That makes it hard to leave. A soul tie is when your soul is knit with another person's soul. We see this in Scripture in 1 Samuel 18:1 (NKJV), "Now when he had finished speaking to Saul, the soul of Jonathan was knit to the soul of David, and Jonathan loved him as his own soul." But witchcraft soul ties are dangerous and can be deadly to your spiritual progress in God.

When charismatic witchcraft prayers are released against you, sickness can attack your body, you can feel worn out all the time even though you are sleeping plenty, your emotions can go haywire for no apparent reason, and you can feel alone and lonely. The good news is you have authority over witchcraft and you can break soul ties by aligning your will with the Lord Jesus Christ, repenting for not discerning the assigning quickly, and renouncing the witchcraft and relationship with charismatic witchcraft practitioners.

It's noteworthy that most of the leaders of The Shepherding Movement later renounced what it became. The movement, at its peak, had 150,000 followers who were under fierce control. Bob Mumford, one of the Fort Lauderdale Five who initiated the movement, was on the cover of *Ministry Today* magazine in January 1990. The words on the cover said, "Discipleship was wrong. I repent. I ask forgiveness." Derek Prince, who also repented, said, "I believe we were guilty of the Galatian error: having begun in the Spirit, we quickly degenerated into the flesh."

Let's all pray that the charismatic witchcraft practitioners will come to repentance because the Bible is clear—they will not inherit eternal life if they continue down this path.

PRAYER

Father, in the name of Jesus, thank You for shedding light on the reality and aim of witchcraft prayers. I repent for any way in which I have tapped into the wrong spirit in my personal prayer life or intercessory prayer ministry. Forgive me, Lord, and help me to discern witchcraft prayers in my midst so I can reverse the ill effects of carnal, fleshly, and even demonic intercession.

NOTES

1. Matthew Henry, *Matthew Henry's Commentary,* s.v. Galatians 5:16, (1706), https://biblehub.com/commentaries/mhc/galatians/5.htm.

2. Matthew Poole, *Matthew Poole's Commentary,* s.v. Galatians 5:21, https://biblehub.com/commentaries/poole/galatians/5.htm.

CHAPTER 10

CONFRONTING JEZEBEL'S INTERCESSORS

It was one of the most difficult meetings I've ever held in my life, but it was time. In fact, it was long overdue. Jezebel-inflicted wounds were literally festering in several women in the congregation, and they finally came forth to expose the depth of the destruction. I only wish they had spoken up sooner.

Let me back up for a moment. There was a woman in our church who was giving, helpful, and there every time the doors were open. But she was out of order more than once—far more than once. She was presumptuous. She stepped into measures of authority that were not delegated to her. She drew people to herself. It was the epitome of Jezebel—and we saw it.

Earlene, as we'll call her, had major issues in her family. Her husband was sickly, her son was addicted to drugs, and her daughter was one of the most insecure young women we'd ever met. We labored long to help the entire family, conducting counseling and engaging in inner healing and deliverance ministry repeatedly. She even sat in the teachings that became the foundation of the book that is in your hands right now, saying "amen" the whole way.

No matter what we tried, how much we prayed, loved, or corrected, the woman would not stop trespassing where she had no authority. But she did change her strategy. She went underground. She started acting like the perfect model of volunteerism while covertly drawing hurting women to herself, telling them she was a deliverance minister and positioning herself as their spiritual mother. Several women in the church told her their deepest, darkest secrets—and somehow, they all believed we sanctioned this despite the reality that she had no public-facing position or authority.

As much as she tried to hide her nefarious motives, others in the congregation started noticing what she did behind closed doors. She set herself up in the lobby to pray for people as they came in, sort of like how Absalom positioned himself at the city gates to woo the people (see 2 Sam. 15:2).

Earlene literally got everyone's phone number who walked in the door and followed up with them to pray, under the guise of performing "greeter duties." She was secretly telling people not to come back to the church because we didn't want them there, didn't care about them, and wouldn't help them. We couldn't be in the sanctuary at the altar and ministering to people and in the lobby at the same time, and she took advantage of this time to work her witchcrafts.

This was indeed the most subtle, underground, wicked Jezebelic attack we had ever seen in the ministry. It wasn't just the icing on the cake; it took the cake, so to speak. And that says a lot since, as a prophetic and prayer ministry, we have perhaps seen more than our fair share of Jezebel attacks over the years. But, as Jesus said in Luke 8:17 (NKJV), "For nothing is secret that will not be revealed, nor anything hidden that will not be known and come to light."

WHEN ENOUGH IS ENOUGH

When several women came to us with matching information—and based on the history we'd already had with Earlene—we knew we had to act swiftly. We called a meeting of the elders to discuss what more we could do to help Earlene. But one of our wisest elders said the best thing we could do is cast her out. She was sowing seeds of discord in the church, which is an abomination. And Proverbs 22:10 (NKJV) tells us, "Cast out the scoffer, and contention will leave; yes, strife and reproach will cease."

By the leadership of the Spirit, we came into agreement that we had already done everything we could to do help this woman and her family—and even her extended family (sisters, cousins, and family friends). She didn't want to be free. She wanted to drive people out of the church, and if she couldn't drive them out she wanted to make eunuchs of them.

Remember, eunuchs were Jezebel's servants. We decided we would confront her as a group of elders Friday night, but monitoring spirits tipped her off. She said she wasn't coming Friday night, but later she did come. We couldn't confront her alone, so we had to put off the confrontation.

The next morning, the Holy Spirit gave me a strategy. Earlene would not deny a personal meeting with me, so I had our office contact her and set up a meeting for Saturday morning. This was a major inconvenience because Saturday is my rest day, but there was no other way. When I drove to the church, I felt like Jehu riding his chariot furiously. I was praying in tongues the whole way there, with a righteous indignation that was set on throwing the spirit of Jezebel down. The plan was to ask Earlene to leave the church, which I had never had to do in over 20 years of ministry.

Since we found out she had a key to the church—a key that was copied without authorization—I purposely told the staff to keep the back door locked and tell her to let herself in so that she would have to use her key. I discerned that otherwise she would claim she forgot her key so that she wouldn't have to give it back. She agreed to come, and I had three staff members as witnesses gathered in the back room. Of course, she purposely didn't bring her key, so we had to let her in.

CONFRONTING JEZEBEL

When she sat down, she seemed nervous since she wasn't expecting three elders to be there with me. I greeted her warmly and thanked her for coming. I told her we had an issue in the church and wanted her to see it. I then pulled out a 30 year-old book from Dick Bernal called *When Lucifer and Jezebel Join Your Church*, and began to read this passage:

> The Jezebel spirit usually operates through women who push themselves off as prophetic. Deep women. Deeper than the pastor. Deeper than God.... The Jezebel spirit uses witchcraft, control, manipulation,

sex, religion, rumor spreading, gossip, false prophecies, etc. This spirit lies at the drop of a hat, digs up one's past, seems overly concerned with leadership in the church, hates male authority, is extremely nosey, bears false witness and loves power....

The woman under this spirit's control wants authority but on her terms only. She usually has a cultic following of dysfunctional women and weak wimpy men. She prays a lot, especially for the pastor and his wife, but her prayers are condescending. She puts herself above the true leadership of the church. Her doctrine is divisive, not building. If she is married, she wears the pants.... If repentance isn't in the picture, the only cure is getting her out of the church and marking her from the pulpit.[1]

With that, I put the book down, looked straight at her and asked, "Who does that sound like to you?" Honestly, I expected her to point out several people in the church whom she had targeted as Jezebels but were not. I expected her to deflect. I expected her to cry and make excuses. But to my shock, Earlene answered, "It sounds like me." I almost had to pick my jaw up off the floor. This was a new strategy, indeed.

At that point, I said, "I'm sorry, but I am going to have to ask you to leave the church. Know that I have not in over 20 years of ministry had to ask someone to leave my church." With that, looking me dead in the eye, she said, "OK." She grabbed her purse and got up to leave, and I said, "Wait a minute." For the next two hours we unraveled the issues around her, all of which she denied. The hope was she would repent, but she refused. She left, mailed the key back, and took about five people with her—her family.

After she left the church, we saw massive growth. We saw stronger believers, including strong young men, come into the congregation with a heart to pray. We saw a radical shift in the worship, and the atmosphere was cleansed. The glory of God began to manifest in a new way. The change was remarkable from the very first week. It was not a comfortable confrontation but a necessary one.

WHY YOU MUST CONFRONT JEZEBEL

Indeed, confrontation is never comfortable, but God confirmed the decision with signs following. If you are a prayer leader, a church leader, a family leader, or the leader of any group in which Jezebel's intercessors have infiltrated, it's your responsibility to confront it.

If you don't confront it, you will open a portal of hell over your group and people will be indoctrinated into the depths of satan, spiritually castrated, and powerless to resist Jezebel—and they will resist your leadership.

It's critical that you remember what Jesus said in Revelation 2:20-23 (NKJV). He was speaking to the church at Thyatira, but He wasn't only speaking to the church at Thyatira. These letters were circulated to other churches and ultimately circulated to us. We need to take heed to what Jesus said:

> *Nevertheless I have a few things against you, because you allow that woman Jezebel, who calls herself a*

> *prophetess, to teach and seduce My servants to commit sexual immorality and eat things sacrificed to idols. And I gave her time to repent of her sexual immorality, and she did not repent.*
>
> *Indeed I will cast her into a sickbed, and those who commit adultery with her into great tribulation, unless they repent of their deeds. I will kill her children with death, and all the churches shall know that I am He who searches the minds and hearts. And I will give to each one of you according to your works.*

That's intense! If you are not confronting, you are tolerating. *Tolerate* means "to allow to be or to be done without prohibition, hindrance, or contradiction." *Tolerate* means to put up with. I promise you, it won't go well for you if you tolerate Jezebel. You can't accept her behavior, condone her control, humor her manipulation, or submit to her seduction.

Many times, the Jezebel spirit can be confronted in the spirit realm, but just as often the person must be confronted face to face. You must use wisdom. You need to be led by the Holy Spirit. There is no cookie-cutter approach here. In my experience, there are three ways to confront Jezebel's intercessors.

First, if you are a believer in a Jezebelic church, know that sometimes confronting looks like leaving. If Jezebel is allowed to run rampant and leadership won't confront it or if the leadership itself is Jezebelic, confronting it face to face likely won't do any good. You'll only start a war you can't fight alone. Remember, Jezebel is not a garden variety demon. Jezebel is a principality that works on the mind.

I HAD TWO CHOICES

I was in a church many years ago that turned Jezebelic. I couldn't believe it because they taught so much about Jezebel. As it turned out, that was just a cover. They were deceived. When I finally accepted the horrifying truth that Jezebel oversaw the organization, I realized I had two choices.

I could pretend I hadn't seen it and continue in my place of authority there, with all my coveted positions, titles, opportunities, front-row seats, dear friends, and various other perks. That was tempting for many reasons, but it was Jezebel tempting me to remain in her nest and, ultimately, I would have lost my prophetic voice. The second option was to be obedient to the revelation the Holy Spirit gave me—and confirmed to me through mature, wise counsel—and walk away.

I was struggling with leaving because it was really the first church that equipped me. I had a soul tie to the place, but it was toxic. I remember lying in my bed asking the Lord what to do? A. Should I talk to the church leadership and explain what I was seeing? B. Should I stay there and just pray for them? C. Should I leave? Many people choose option B. They convince themselves they should stay and pray. But that's almost always the wrong decision. You can pray for them from the outside. You don't need sit under Jezebel's authority. If you do, you will wind up deceived.

So what did I do? Well, the Holy Spirit told me to forgive them all for everything they had done to me. I must have spent a half hour forgiving all the wrong they had done. When I couldn't remember anything else to forgive, the Holy Spirit said, "Now go in peace."

In other words, don't tell everyone why you are leaving. Just go. That's what I did. I told my life group leader, and she relayed the message to the heads of the church. I was willing to speak to the leaders about the issue, even though that was a terrifying prospect. But the leaders did not want to speak with me. Keep in mind I was one of the most visible people in the church, one of the largest donors. I was running their entire media department and teaching weekly. You would think they would have wanted to talk to me. They just let me walk away because that spirit on them knew I saw it and would not bow.

WHY IT'S HARD TO LEAVE

As I wrote in my book *The Spiritual Warrior's Guide to Defeating Jezebel*, part of the reason why the decision was so agonizing was because I knew I would face tremendous persecution when I left. I had seen others leave Jezebel's den. They were colored with the brush of deception, accused of flowing in hurts, wounds, rejection—and even a Jezebel spirit.

I didn't want to endure that persecution, but I finally decided that I could obey what the Holy Spirit showed me or relinquish myself to spiritual delusion. The Holy Spirit had opened a door— and He told me to go in peace. To stay would have been to disobey. I shudder to think what fate I may have suffered in this age and the age to come had the Holy Spirit not graced me to obey.

Just as I feared, when I walked away, I was sorely persecuted by the Jezebel spirit working through the very people I had co-labored with for so many years. Mature believers watching from the outside called it psychological warfare and emotional terrorism. Those descriptions fit. I learned that you can only submit to one spirit at a time. In other words, you can't submit to the Holy Spirit and submit to the Jezebel spirit at once. You must choose. But when you choose the Holy Spirit, God's glory will rest upon you.

Yes, my decision to refuse to bow to any hint of that Jezebel spirit unleashed a war against me that I had never experienced before. After all, the organization had to protect its reputation. Because I was a high-profile member of the group, and because I was not allowed to offer a reason for my departure, all manner of lies were seeded to the group about me. I was suddenly positioned as rebellious, deceived, prideful—and a Jezebel. It was one of the most confusing periods of my life and I did a lot of soul searching. I submitted myself to many Christian leaders for examination.

Over and over again, I was found "not guilty" of the accusations. And over and over again confirmations came that I had done the right thing. Within months after I left the organization, others started leaving and told me that they found courage to escape the clutches of this Jezebelic organization after I was bold enough to walk away—and walk away without launching a public attack on my accusers (or even responding to their public accusations). In fact, I was told time and time again that the public attacks against me were so vitriolic that it only confirmed who was really flowing in the wrong spirit—and it wasn't me.

I said all that to say this: Within months of confronting Jezebel, God began restoring all the things that I gave up in order to follow Him. And not only did He restore them, He gave me positions and opportunities and other perks that far surpassed those things from which I had walked away. I could tick down a list for you. But what it boils down to is authority. Jesus gave me a greater sphere of authority and influence than I could have imagined. He began to fulfill prophetic words and dreams from years ago in rapid-fire succession.

Whereas Jezebel tried to shut down my voice by discrediting me, Jesus opened the doors of utterance among the nations. Today, I have hundreds of prayer hub leaders in dozens of nations on several continents through Awakening Prayer Hubs (www.awakeningprayerhubs.com). If I had not been willing to leave a Jezebelic stronghold, I would have become a eunuch and missed my high calling.

CONFRONT JEZEBEL IN THE SPIRIT

You can also confront Jezebel in the spirit. Sometimes Jezebel's intercessors will come to a prayer meeting just to spy. Paul the apostle says it this way:

> *And this occurred because of false brethren secretly brought in (who came in by stealth to spy out our liberty which we have in Christ Jesus, that they might bring us into bondage)* (Galatians 2:4 NKJV).

When Jezebel's intercessors act as spies in undercover mode, they aren't praying on the mic—but they are releasing witchcraft and looking for people to prey upon. They are scouting out the land. If Jezebel's intercessor is keeping a low profile, you may not discern them immediately. You may not know where the witchcraft you're sensing is coming from, but you can discern the witchcraft. That's when you deal with it in the spirit.

Likewise, you may not have the opportunity to speak to the person who's operating in the Jezebel spirit. Many times, they slip out before the end of a service or avoid the leadership. We've seen this happen time and time again. You can still deal with it in the spirit. Remember, we're not wrestling against flesh and blood but against a principality that has someone's mind in bondage.

The Passion Translation of Ephesians 6:12 puts it this way:

> *Your hand-to-hand combat is not with human beings, but with the highest principalities and authorities operating in rebellion under the heavenly realms. For they are a powerful class of demon-gods and evil spirits that hold this dark world in bondage.*

The Message voices it in a different tone:

> *This is no weekend war that we'll walk away from and forget about in a couple of hours. This is for keeps, a life-or-death fight to the finish against the Devil and all his angels.*

Our war with Jezebel is not a war with a personality. It's a war with a principality. In other words, the person is not your enemy. The spirit is.

Remember, we're dealing with a hurt and wounded person who has given their will over to Jezebel. If Jezebel's intercessor is not a person you know well and have no spiritual authority over, it can be most strategic to shut it down in the spirit.

What do I mean by that? I mean pray and bind that spirit. Forbid Jezebel's intercessors from walking through the threshold unless the person is seeking freedom and wants to submit to spiritual authority. We've been successful using this strategy to make a clean break.

CONFRONTING JEZEBEL IN CONVERSATION

Sometimes, Jezebel's intercessor needs to be confronted in a strong conversation. That's what we did with Earlene. But you need to be prepared for this level of confrontation. In the case with Earlene, it went differently than I thought. Though she defended herself, she didn't react in the typical Jezebelic manner. In most cases, you need to do the following.

First, spend time in prayer. Check your own heart to make sure you are not making a false accusation or your discernment is not off. You don't want to try to take the speck out of someone's eye when you have a telephone pole in your own eye (see Matt. 7:5). We don't want to be hypocrites. We want to be holy in our confrontation, so we need to examine ourselves to find any biases that would lead us to false accusations.

If you are not the leader, you should share what you are seeing with a leader rather than confronting it yourself. Even if you are part of the confrontation, you will need a leader who has spiritual authority with you if you are going to directly call someone out for operating in a Jezebel spirit. If you take this on alone, you will either bring warfare on yourself that you may not have the grace to handle or you may find leadership rebuking you for interfering with their own plans to confront Jezebel. Don't usurp the leader's authority. Remember, that's what Jezebel does.

Before you confront the person, write down the Jezebelic behaviors in which they are operating. Document this in writing before the conversation. Get as specific as possible. In most cases, Jezebel will argue with you, deflect, act hurt, and cry crocodile tears to gain your sympathy.

WARNING: DON'T FEEL SORRY FOR JEZEBEL

If you feel sorry for Jezebel, she'll not only pull on your heart strings, but she'll play you like the proverbial fiddle. This master manipulator will seduce you into her web of witchcraft using your own compassion as bait.

People influenced by a Jezebel spirit play the victim. They want your pity. The reason this seducing spirit wants your sympathy is strategic: Pity opens the door for this devil. Soulish compassion blocks discernment—but that's no excuse for tolerating Jezebel. In fact, if you tolerate a Jezebel spirit, Jesus has something against you. Jesus has made a pathway for people in bondage to Jezebel to repent, but our soulish compassion will not lead someone to repentance. Jezebel knows this and teaches her prey to play the victim so you'll feel sorry for them and tolerate the ungodly behavior.

Most people operating in a Jezebel spirit have a long, sad story of how they've been sorely abused; how people misunderstand them; how they've been falsely accused; how they've lived a lifetime of sickness; how churches mistreat them—or some other tall tale they remind you of as often as you'll listen. They want to form a codependent relationship with you so you can pet their flesh—and they can pet yours. The entire scene is sad, truly sad. But offering soulish compassion is just a manifestation of tolerating Jezebel.

CHRIST'S COMPASSION LEADS TO MIRACLES

We must not tolerate Jezebel's tactics. We cannot come into agreement with somebody's self-pity. Self-pity attracts devils. Many of us go through trauma and tragedy in our lives. We have two choices—submit our broken soul to the Holy Spirit so He can pour out the healing balm of Gilead or harden our hearts, choose unforgiveness, and invite demons to erect strongholds in our minds.

Those operating in a Jezebel spirit chose the latter, even if they didn't understand what they were choosing. They are carrying unresolved hurts and wounds that opened the door for Jezebel to serve as a guardian when Jesus was there the whole time with outstretched arms willing to heal.

It's a tragic reality, but it doesn't have to be. People influenced by a Jezebel spirit can choose to break free—but it's a choice only they can make. We need to have Christ's compassion on people operating in a Jezebel spirit, and that means refusing to play patty-cake with demons, standing strong against this spirit's manipulation and control tactics, speaking the truth in love, and refusing to feel sorry for Jezebel.

We cannot tolerate this spirit for a moment. We need to point those influenced by this seducing devil to the truth that sets them free (see John 8:32). Jesus is the truth (see John 14:6). The entrance of His Word brings light (see Ps. 119:130). Ultimately, you can only labor so long with someone who flat-out refuses to face the pain that led them to trust a spirit other than the Holy Spirit to protect them. Ultimately, if Jezebel won't repent, you have to pull back and pray. Let the Spirit of God lead you, but remember this: Jesus will never lead you to tolerate Jezebel.

Pray and ask God for a strategy to confront Jezebel's intercessors. God loves the person and hates the enemy. You can be gracious with the person; you can't be gracious with the spirit. Address it how the Holy Spirit shows you. But be sure to address it as quickly as possible. Time is not on your side. The longer you don't confront it, the more damage it can do. What's more, when you tolerate that spirit, Jesus has issues with you. It opens a portal of hell over your life.

Jesus said in Revelation 2 that if Jezebel doesn't repent, He will throw her on a sickbed and those who commit adultery with her. Sometimes you have to cast the demon out of a person. But sometimes you have to cast the person out of the church.

PRAYER

Father, in the name of Jesus, would You give me the wisdom and courage to confront Jezebelic intercessors? Give me the words to speak to shed light on the lies. Help me to speak that truth in love that breaks yokes. I want to restore people in a spirit of gentleness rather than causing more harm. Help me know when my efforts toward restoration are exhausted and people must move on for the sake of Your mission.

NOTE

1. Dick Bernal, *When Lucifer and Jezebel Join Your Church* (Jubilee Christian Center, 1994), 24.

CHAPTER 11

DEALING WITH JEZEBEL'S
AFTERMATH

Eighty thousand people were instantly killed when the United States dropped an atomic bomb on Hiroshima in 1945. Thirteen square kilometers of the city were reduced to rubble in the blink of an eye. Three days later, another atomic bomb landed on Nagasaki, killing another 40,000 people.

In the aftermath of the atomic bombs, the two Japanese cities were on fire and unrecognizable, but so were the dead people in the city. Wilfred Burchett, an Australian journalist who was the first foreign correspondent to enter Hiroshima after the bomb, said this: "Hundreds and hundreds of the dead were so badly burned in the terrific heat generated by the bomb that it was not even possible to tell whether they were men or women, old or young."

Those who didn't die immediately suffered severe radiation poisoning and would die in the months ahead. Indeed, the death toll climbed to 130,000 by the end of 1945. Those who survived radiation poisoning were thought to be contagious and shunned, facing tremendous financial hardship. Indeed, so great was the destruction that Albert Einstein said, "If I had foreseen Hiroshima and Nagasaki, I would have torn up my formula in 1905."

JEZEBEL'S AFTERMATH EXPOSED

An aftermath is defined as the period immediately following a usually ruinous event. When Jezebel's intercessors are not nipped in the bud, the aftermath will often be so great that it seems like a spiritual bomb has gone off in your midst. Sometimes even when you deal with the issues swiftly, there's an aftermath—even if it's not immediately visible. Indeed, sometimes there's a calm before the storm.

I've learned the aftermath of a Jezebel attack in a church or business often ripples for about a year. You find out more and more about who was cooperating, who was hurt, and who still has Jezebelic seeds in their soul. In other words, the clean-up process is not an afternoon project. Seeds take a while to bear fruit. And if the seeds aren't rooted out, the fruit will spring forth in the next season.

We need to stay on the alert—not in paranoia, but alert—because Jezebel is roaming about like a roaring lion seeking someone to devour (see 1 Pet. 5:8). Some newly minted Jezebels make a stink on the way out the door. More mature—or high-level—Jezebels are more cunning and calculating. They wait for the opportune time to strike (see Luke 4:13). The opportune time is when you put your guard down. The opportune time is when you least expect it. The opportune time is when you are already under attack.

We saw this happen with Earlene. When I confronted Earlene with the facts of her behavior, reminded her of how many times she'd been taught, counseled, corrected, walked through inner healing and deliverance, she left without much fanfare. The next Sunday, her whole family was still in church as if nothing happened. We were glad to see them but were waiting for the other shoe to drop.

Eventually, most of the family left except her brother. Her brother had told us many times over two years that Earlene was a controlling manipulator. Even though it was hard for him to deal with Earlene's urgings to leave the church, he decided to stay on. He was grateful for the spiritual growth in his life, and didn't want to follow his sister's lead. He stayed on for a season but then eventually concocted a detailed story about some training and left quietly. It was all lies. He lied his way out the door because down deep inside he was too ashamed to tell the truth.

We knew Earlene had been sowing seeds into the hearts of many women in the ministry, but we didn't know the depth of it. Several women left the church over the next few months and subsequently drew others out as well. But the church, nevertheless, was growing by leaps and bounds. It was like the atmosphere was cleared out and winds of refreshing were blowing.

ATHALIAH RISING

We thought that was the end of it, until Athaliah rose up. Jezebel's eggs started hatching in one of the younger women, Janie. Her husband had walked in a spirit of offense off and on since they came to the church, but Janie was hungry for spiritual growth and was progressing.

Eventually, though, her husband's offense wore her down and she bowed to him. What a shame it is to watch people compromise with demons. But Janie also reproduced herself in Carla. Then Carla reproduced herself in Maggie. It was Jezebel's revenge. The following is an excerpt from my book *Jezebel's Revenge*:

Who is Athaliah? This spirit is not much talked about—and she likes it that way. Demons are neither male nor female, but I call Athaliah she just because this spirit worked most predominantly through a female in the Bible. However, let's be clear: Like Jezebel, Athaliah can work through a male or female.

Athaliah has stayed under the radar screen of mainline spiritual warriors. But make no mistake, while many still have a hard time believing there is a real Jezebel spirit, the spirit of Athaliah is gaining momentum and wreaking real havoc on the lives of those who don't see her. The hour has come when Athaliah is rising and attacking at new levels. Ignorance of this demon will bring much destruction to churches, families, and lives.

I hadn't heard much teaching on Athaliah when I bumped into this demon—and I haven't heard much teaching on it since. Again, Athaliah likes it that way. If she can stay hidden in the shadows—if she can keep us ignorant to her existence—she can operate without much resistance. But our ignorance does not make us immune to the reality of this stealth satanic agent. It's a lie that ignorance is bliss. In fact, ignorance could be deadly. That's why Paul warned us not to be ignorant of the devil's devices.

Second Corinthians 2:11 (AMPC) tells us, "For we are not ignorant of his wiles and intentions." The New Living Translation puts it this way: "For we are familiar with his evil schemes." *The Message* says, "We're not oblivious to his sly ways." And The Passion

Translation emotes, "For we know his clever schemes." Athaliah, like other demon powers, has wicked wiles, infuriating intentions, evil schemes, sly ways, and clever manipulations. The agenda of any demon is to steal, kill, and destroy (see John 10:10). Athaliah goes about it a little differently than some other spiritual enemies.

Practically speaking, here's one way you bump into this spirit. Let's say you find yourself in a battle with Jezebel. You enter into a spiritual wrestling match. You employ the skills you've learned and execute your spiritual authority and throw Jezebel down. You gain the victory. Then, seemingly out of nowhere Athaliah strikes.

You may think you didn't defeat Jezebel and reemploy the same strategy, trying to push Jezebel back again. But that doesn't work because you're not dealing with Jezebel anymore. You made a presumption in the spirit and you're growing battle weary. You're really dealing with Athaliah, who looks a lot like Jezebel but is not. You can't come against Jezebel without experiencing revenge from Jezebel's daughter.

Battling Athaliah takes a different strategy. Again, it's not the same spirit. Again, Athaliah looks a lot like Jezebel. Athaliah may act a lot like Jezebel. But Athaliah is not Jezebel

According to *Smith's Bible Dictionary*, the name *Athaliah* means "afflicted of the Lord," and *Easton's Bible Dictionary* defines the name as "whom God afflicts." That seems like a fitting name for a daughter of this wicked queen. But it gives you a hint—God always sees Athaliah as a defeated foe.

The Lord sees all our enemies as defeated foes. That's because Jesus triumphed over them on the cross. Colossians 2:15 (NKJV) reads, "Having disarmed principalities and powers, He made a public spectacle of them, triumphing over them in it." However, we must enforce Christ's victory with His powerful name and delegated authority.

Pulpit Commentary tells us, "We find in this woman, Athaliah, the infernal tendencies of her father and her mother, Ahab and Jezebel. Though they had been swept as monsters from the earth, and were now lying in the grave, their hellish spirit lived and worked in this their daughter. It is, alas! often so. We have an immortality in others, as well as in ourselves. The men of long-forgotten generations still live in the present. Even the moral pulse of Adam throbs in all."[1]

What does the spirit of Athaliah look like in action? I go way deeper in my book *Jezebel's Revenge*. But to give you a quick summary: Athaliah is a murdering, self-advancing spirit—much like Jezebel but perhaps even more vicious. You need discernment in this battle because, at first glance, Athaliah looks like Jezebel.

I can't stress that enough. You need to know your enemy before you can truly defeat your enemy. You don't want to, as Paul said, beat the air (see 1 Cor. 9:26). And you don't want to pick a fight with a demon that's not bothering you. Like me, I'm sure you have enough warfare without stirring up devils that don't have you on their radar screen. Learn more about Athaliah in my book *Jezebel's Revenge*.

ENCOURAGE YOURSELF IN THE LORD

The Philistine kings just rejected David's participation in their battle against Israel. David and his men headed back to Ziklag, their allotted land behind enemy lines. When they arrived, they discovered the Amalekites had invaded Ziklag, burned it with fire and taken the women and children captive (see 1 Sam. 30:1-2).

David and all his men wept until they had no more power to weep. David was stressed out because the men who followed him loyally through the wilderness blamed him. In their grief over losing their families, David's troops had talks about stoning him. David turned and strengthened himself in the Lord his God (see 1 Sam. 30:6). Some versions say he encouraged himself in the Lord.

When you see Jezebel's aftermath, it's discouraging. In the blink of an eye, it seems Jezebel's intercessors can tear down what it took you years to build. You may feel like giving up. Don't give Jezebel the satisfaction. Understand she came to steal, kill, and destroy but God can restore and help you build back better. Turn away from the trauma Jezebel inflicted and encourage yourself by looking at Jesus.

RALLY THE TROOPS

Once you've caught your breath and regained some strength, rally the troops. That's what David did. He consulted the Lord, asking if he should go after the enemy that pillaged his land and kidnapped his people. The Lord told him, "Pursue, for you shall surely overtake them and without fail recover all" (1 Sam. 30:8 NKJV). David gathered troops and marched into enemy territory to take back what the enemy stole.

We're not talking about going after the people Jezebel's intercessors took out. If Jezebel's intercessors were able to take them out, they probably had common ground with Jezebel and they, too, would eventually become a proverbial thorn in your side. It's better to see a clean sweep than continual drama that produces a toxic culture. Unless the Holy Spirit instructs you, don't go after those who left. Just pray that they will break ties with evil influences that will sabotage their lives.

Remember what John the Beloved said, "These people left our churches, but they never really belonged with us; otherwise they would have stayed with us. When they left, it proved that they did not belong with us" (1 John 2:19 NLT). What you see as a spiritual attack is often the Lord allowing the enemy to remove people who are hindering your assignment because they won't repent.

That said, this is a spiritual battle. Rally the troops to close any open doors. Rally the troops to uproot any additional Jezebelic influences in your midst. Rally the troops to plead the blood of Jesus over the minds of those who are on the fence about staying or leaving based on what was said to them. Rally the troops against the spirit of seduction that woos people away from the truth.

STRENGTHEN WHAT REMAINS

Jesus said in Revelation 3:2 (NKJV), "Be watchful, and strengthen the things which remain." Strengthen what remains—not what you lost. The word *strengthen* in that verse comes from the Greek word *sterizo*, which means "to make stable, place firmly, set fast, fix, strengthen, and to make one's mind constant."

Jezebel's intercessors may still be talking to people in your church. She may still be laying eggs in people's souls. Remember, Jezebel looks for the unstable—the hurt and wounded. One of Earlene's cronies started contacting people at our church, one by one, and asking them to urgently contact her. She had never even spoken to many of the people she targeted when she was at the church, but she was on a mission to steal, kill, and destroy. The first step to strengthening what remains is to pray. Pray that Jezebel's plots are exposed. Pray that people will see the truth, because the truth sets them free (see John 8:2).

If people were wounded at the hand of Jezebel's intercessors, take the time to pray with them. If they need answers, do the best you can to provide them. Show them what the Bible says about what you just experienced. The entrance of His word brings light (see Ps. 119:130). If they need inner healing or deliverance, make a way for it.

Another way to strengthen what remains is to set stronger protocols in place. I didn't say control. I said protocols. Sometimes people don't know what the etiquette in your church is. For example, what are the protocols for the prayer meeting, for the release of prophecy, and so on?

If people don't know the protocol, they won't know when someone is out of order. Jezebel's intercessors will violate them even if they know them—and play dumb as they do it. When you teach your community the protocols, they can clearly see who is intentionally violating them and who just needs to be made aware of how things are done in your group.

DON'T CLOSE YOUR HEART

Be careful not to close your heart. People always ask me how I remain so open to people even though I've been betrayed so many times. I remain open because I'm called to minister to people. I can't minister from a closed heart. If I shut out people, I may eventually find myself shutting out God Himself. If I seek to protect myself from the pain of betrayal, I shut Him out as my protector.

If you've been betrayed or harmed by Jezebel's intercessors, you have to forgive. The Holy Spirit told me once, "Trust in the Lord and do good." Listen to some of the rest of this psalm and let it encourage your heart from Psalm 37:1-9 (MEV):

> *Do not fret because of evildoers, nor be jealous of those who do injustice. For they will quickly wither like the grass, and fade like the green herbs. Trust in the Lord, and do good; dwell in the land, and practice faithfulness. Delight yourself in the Lord, and He will give you the desires of your heart.*
>
> *Commit your way to the Lord; trust also in Him, and He will bring it to pass. He will bring forth your righteousness as the light, and your judgment as the noonday. Rest in the Lord, and wait patiently for Him; do not fret because of those who prosper in their way, because of those who make wicked schemes. Let go of anger, and forsake wrath; do not fret—it surely leads to evil deeds. For evildoers will be cut off, but those who hope in the Lord will inherit the earth.*

I don't know about you, but that changes everything for me. God is our vindicator. We can't always trust people, but we can certainly always trust Him. Don't close your heart to people. That's just what Jezebel wants.

DEBRIEF AFTER THE BATTLE

It's important to debrief after a battle. Every time you walk through a war, debrief. Debriefings originated in the military. A debriefing is just a review of what went right, what went wrong, and what we could do better next time. We want to understand how the enemy worked, how God worked, how we worked against ourselves, and how we ultimately got the victory.

Do your debriefing with the Holy Spirit and with others who walked closely with you through the battle. Ask yourself questions like: How did Jezebel get in? Why didn't we discern this assignment? How should we have been praying? What can we do differently next time? What have we learned that will help us the next time Jezebel's intercessors infiltrate?

DON'T MAKE FALSE JEZEBEL ACCUSATIONS

When you've sustained attacks from Jezebel's intercessors, it can be easy to mislabel anything that smells even a little like Jezebel as Jezebel. This is a mistake. I've been part of churches where people are labeled Jezebels shortly after they walk in the door. They were marked with a scarlet letter as controllers and manipulators who want to get close to the pastor for power and position.

The reality is they may be controllers and manipulators, or they may not be. The real controllers and manipulators are more often, in my experience, the ones slinging the misguided Jezebel accusations. Along with "false prophet," a Jezebel accusation is one of the most serious fiery darts you can throw at a believer. It implies that they aren't a believer at all but that they are fornicators who will not inherit the Kingdom of God and false brethren who are purposefully leading people away from Christ for their own gain.

PRAYER

Father, in the name of Jesus, I repent for wrong moves or lack of action I took that may have allowed Jezebel's intercessors in or made room for this spirit to entrench itself into the prayer ministry. Please forgive me. Help me learn from this experience so that I don't make the same mistakes again. Help me to continue to believe the best about people without missing Your warnings. Would You help me to clean up the mess Jezebel made and strengthen what remains?

NOTE

1. D. Thomas, *Pulpit Commentary*, "The History of Athaliah," https://biblehub.com/sermons/auth/thomas/the_history_of_athaliah.htm.

CHAPTER 12

WHAT JEZEBEL'S INTERCESSORS DON'T WANT YOU TO KNOW

I cut my teeth in Christianity at a church that knew Jezebel from the inside out. Or at least they claimed to. The head pastor positioned himself as an "expert" on Jezebel. I always thought that was a dangerous claim because it was rooted in pride—and that bravado got Jezebel's attention. The church is a shell of what it was and the leader's influence, which was once ascending, has crumbled.

With that in mind, I don't claim to be an expert on the Jezebel spirit or Jezebel's intercessors. But through knowledge of Jezebel's intercessors, the study of God's Word, and the many attacks on Awakening House of Prayer, my church in South Florida, I've learned a thing or two. Indeed, I've learned many truths about Jezebel's intercessors that Jezebel doesn't want me to know. But it's too late.

If knowledge is power, and it is a form of power as we are not to be ignorant of the devil's devices, the knowledge I am going to share about Jezebel and her intercessors in this chapter will supercharge your spiritual warfare skills (see 2 Cor. 2:11). Like I always say, an enemy exposed is an enemy defeated. The following are questions I studied out for myself, as well as questions other people have asked me over the years.

What is the spirit of Jezebel?

First let's talk about what the spirit of Jezebel is not, because there are a lot of false Jezebel accusations out there. Jezebel is not a woman with a strong personality who just needs some people skills.

Jezebel is not a spirit of control or a spirit of manipulation. Jezebel uses control and manipulation as a means to an end. But if you look at control and manipulation, or even the hunt for power, as the end of the story then you are missing the heart of the matter.

Jezebel is a spirit of seduction and it's running rampant in the world and in the church. Remember, Jesus pointed out the purpose of Jezebel in Revelation 2:20—to teach and seduce. *Seduce* in that verse comes from the Greek word *planao*, which means "to cause to stray, to lead astray, to lead aside from the right way, to lead away from the truth, to lead into error, to deceive, to be led away into error or sin," according to *The KJV New Testament Greek Lexicon*.

Jezebel wants to lead, but she will lead you into the depths of satan.

What does the name Jezebel mean?

In the ancient world, names carried more meaning than they do today. When God changed Abram's name to Abraham and Jacob's name to Israel, it carried significance. Likewise, when Jesus changed Simon's name to Peter and when Saul's name was changed to Paul, it was purposeful.

So what does the name *Jezebel* mean in Hebrew? *BDB Theological Dictionary* defines it as "un-exalted or un-husbanded." Clearly, Queen Jezebel had a husband, but it seems she wore the pants in the family. *Jones' Dictionary of Old Testament Proper Names* defines Jezebel as without cohabitation. Cohabitation is living together or in a company, or to exist together. Jezebel doesn't want to share her power or authority and won't submit to any power or authority.

Of course, we also see a Jezebel in Revelation 2:20. The name Jezebel is a "symbolic name of a woman who pretended to be a prophetess, and who, addicted to antinomianism, claimed Christian liberty of eating things sacrificed to idols," according to *Thayer's Greek Lexicon*.

Antinomianism is a doctrine that essentially gives Christians a grace license to sin. *Merriam-Webster's Dictionary* defines it as "one who rejects a socially established morality." Basically, it means we can live however we want if we have faith in Christ. It's heretical, and part of the depths of satan Jesus described in Revelation 2.

Why do we call this spirit Jezebel? Is that what God calls it?

We use the name *Jezebel* because the two women in Scripture who carried the name had much in common. We use it as a common descriptor. I do not believe there is a spirit named Jezebel, per se. What we're dealing with here, again, is a spirit of seduction. Jezebel served the goddess of Ashtoreth. But we use Jezebel in the way that doctors around the world use the name *cancer*. We need a common name by which to identify this deadly enemy.

Why are there two Jezebels in Scripture?

I believe there are two Jezebels in Scripture to demonstrate that this spirit has been wreaking havoc on God's people—first the prophets in the Old Testament and later in the end times—for centuries. Lester Sumrall said the Jezebel spirit would be one of the main opponents of the church in the end times. It's no accident we see the rise of this spirit and Jesus' warning and rebuke in the Book of Revelation.

Why does Jezebel hate prophets and intercessors?

Jezebel hates prophets and intercessors because they carry the voice and release the power of God through prayer. Jezebel knows prayer is our lifeline to God and will stop at nothing to control our prayer or stop us from praying. Remember, she cut off the prophets of the Lord (see 1 Kings 18:4). She wants to cut off the intercessors too.

Can a Christian have a Jezebel spirit?

A Christian can be influenced by what we call the Jezebel spirit, but I do not believe you can cast out Jezebel, which is a name we use for what is really Ashtoreth. Again, Ashtoreth is a principality and principalities do not inhabit the bodies of people. They reign in the second heaven.

Principalities influence the minds of people, which opens them up to other demons, such as the spirit of seduction. But Jezebel doesn't take up residence in believers. What we call Jezebel is essentially a spirit of seduction. You can cast out the spirit of seduction, which often enters through hurts, wounds, and rejection. Find out more in my course Deliverance from the Jezebel Spirit at www.schoolofthespirit.tv.

Do you see the spirit of Jezebel rising in this hour?

Yes, though I believe Jezebel has been rising for centuries. We just didn't have much teaching on the topic until the 1990s. I believe we've been battling this principality in cities and nations all over the world, but we didn't have a name for it. We didn't know it was Jezebel, or more accurately Ashtoreth.

What is Jezebel's master plan?

The spirit of Jezebel is dangerous on several levels. Jezebel wants to seduce you away from your first love.

Jesus issued one of the strongest rebukes found in the New Testament against the church at Thyatira for tolerating Jezebel. In Revelation 2:20 (NKJV), Jesus says:

> *I have a few things against you, because you allow that woman Jezebel, who calls herself a prophetess, to teach and seduce My servants to commit sexual immorality and eat things sacrificed to idols.*

Jezebel pushes out a distorted grace message. She tells you it's OK to commit adultery, to fornicate, to engage in homosexual relationships. She tells you it's OK to put other things before God, which is idolatry. Jezebel seduces you into sexual immorality and idolatry with her false doctrine. She assures you it's OK to sin in these ways and still come sing on the praise team, or still come work in kid's church. And it's not OK.

When we sin, we can repent. But Jezebel's doctrine does not require repentance. Jesus gave Jezebel space to repent and she would not. And she teaches her followers that they don't have to repent either. This is a doctrine of demons.

Jesus calls Jezebel's doctrine the depths of satan in Revelation 2:24. Look at all the high-profile scandals in the church where pastors are having affairs—even homosexual affairs—and all the financial impropriety. Pastors can't blame Jezebel for falling into adultery but be assured Jezebel was involved in wooing them into immorality. That doesn't take the responsibility off pastors or anyone else. The Bible tells us not to be ignorant of the devil's devices.

Jezebel's ultimate motive is not to control you. Jezebel's ultimate motive is to destroy you.

Jesus said He would cast Jezebel on a sickbed, and those who commit adultery with her into great tribulation unless they repent of their deeds. Jesus said in Revelation 2:23 (NKJV):

> *I will kill her children with death* [her children are those who follow her teachings], *and all the churches shall know that I am He who searches the minds and*

hearts. And I will give to each one of you according to your works.

What is the origin of the Jezebel spirit in Scripture?

Jezebel and Babylon have a long history with one another. Generally, the Jezebel spirit is first identified in the Old Testament queen for whom it is named. But the spirit that influenced Queen Jezebel was alive and well long before she personified many of its traits.

The beginning of Nimrod's kingdom was the city of Babel. Bible historians conclude that Nimrod led the Tower of Babel project in the land of Shinar. It was an act of rebellion.

Nimrod married a pagan woman named Semiramis. That is where Nimrod's Babylonian story takes a Jezebelic twist. Semiramis was also known as Ishtar or the Queen of Heaven. Semiramis has many of the same characteristics as Queen Jezebel. She is the one who introduced sexual immorality into the pagan religion. In fact, Jezebel is also known as Ishtar or the Queen of Heaven. Semiramis exhibited the first recorded manifestation of what we call Jezebel.

Semiramis, who had boasted of being a virgin queen, became pregnant after Nimrod's death. By coming up with a clever story, she found a way both to cover her immorality and to deify her late husband: She declared that the spirit of Nimrod had gotten her pregnant.

Semiramis' son, who was named Tammuz, was introduced as a reincarnated Nimrod and positioned as a god. Semiramis soon became the mother of a cult that claimed divine wisdom, but, like the Jezebel of the book of Revelation, she taught her followers to serve idols and to commit sexual immorality. Semiramis promoted a perverted trinity—herself, Nimrod, and Tammuz.

Many people still think Jezebel is just a controlling woman or even a spirit of control. Why is there so much confusion over what the Jezebel spirit really is?

I believe it's because we look too much at flesh, which manifests control, and we look too much at the surface-level fruits of Jezebel. Jezebel uses control and manipulation, but Jezebel hides behind the branches of these other spirits.

We've had an incomplete revelation of Jezebel. Talk of Jezebel started many years ago with a single book, then other people picked up on the truth in that book and began to parrot it. But fewer are digging deeper into Scripture to pull back the veil.

Also, you'll hear a lot of extra-biblical talk about Jezebel. This is dangerous. People claim to be Jezebel experts. You can type "spirit of Jezebel" into Google and you'll get about 5.2 million results in less than a quarter of a second.

Much of what you read is hype and rubbish. They speak from their personal experience without scriptural backing and have come out with some outlandish conclusions and characteristics of Jezebel. And it's further deceiving people. Jezebel laughs because we don't see her. We're focused on control.

Can we ever truly get rid of Jezebel?

We'll never completely tear down Jezebel until Jesus returns. But we can stop this spirit from operating in our own lives and families—if we know what it really is.

How does the spirit of Jezebel manifest through a believer?

It depends on how much influence Jezebel is exerting in a believer's life. I subscribe to the late Dr. Lester Sumrall's theory of demon possession he writes about in his classic *Demonology and Deliverance* series. That goes from regression all the way to possession.

Since Jezebel is most successful working through people with hurts or wounds, it often starts with a believer making a pact with Jezebel that sounds something like this: "I will never let them hurt me again" or "From now on, nobody is going to tell me what I can and can't do." Jezebel takes that as an invitation and will come in to protect you. She does this by making suggestions to your soul, which often results in backsliding into some form of sin or another with justification.

From there, Jezebel begins to pressure one's emotions so they overreact when a person taps into an old unhealed wound.

What is the fruit of the Jezebel spirit?

At the surface level—and from my practical experience dealing with this spirit—the fruit of the Jezebel spirit includes control, manipulation, flattery, strife, defensiveness, pride, dishonesty, ungratefulness, a critical spirit, over-competitiveness, intimidation, super-spiritualism, pushiness, attention-seeking, vengefulness, disapproval, over-ambition, independence, disdain for authority, position-seeking, lust, hunger for power, and a religious spirit. But just because you see these traits in people doesn't automatically make them a Jezebel. And it's dangerous to make a false accusation like that.

What's the difference between true spiritual authority and false authority?

If you are born again, then you have keys to the Kingdom—whatever you bind on earth is bound in heaven and whatever you loose on earth is loosed in heaven (see Matt. 18:18). You have authority. Jesus gave you authority.

What you do with that authority is vital. When you use God's Word the way God wills, He is inclined to give you more opportunities. When you do not use God's Word God's way—such as to bring increase to the Kingdom, to comfort those who mourn, to edify people—He is inclined to take those opportunities and give them to someone who ministers His purpose more faithfully. This concept is illustrated in Jesus' Parable of the Sower (see Matt. 13).

Much the same, I believe that when we misuse our authority, or we are not willing to exercise it according to God's will, we open the door to the enemy. Sometimes that enemy is named Jezebel. Jezebel cannot fully accomplish her work in this realm, however, without a physical body. Jezebel wants to use yours and mine to get her dirty work done. Jezebel wants to usurp our authority but cannot do it forcibly. We must hand our authority over.

We know that all true spiritual authority comes from our loving Jesus. Jezebel, by contrast, walks in false authority—unlawful rulership that she usurps. It was the Old Testament Queen Jezebel who proclaimed to her husband, "You now exercise authority over Israel!" and then proceeded to write letters in King Ahab's name, seal them with his seal, and send them to do her bidding.

True spiritual authority refuses to tolerate the work of the enemy and refuses to violate the law of love. True authority puts on the whole armor of God to wrestle against principalities and powers, including Jezebel, but never forgets that the armor is more than a sword alone.

Righteousness, truth, faith, and peace are essential to walking in true spiritual authority. When you compromise in those areas, you compromise your efficacy against principalities and powers. People flowing in a Jezebel spirit walk in false authority—or they abuse the authority they have.

Can you tell me about one of your battles against the spirit of Jezebel?

I was in a church one time where Jezebel was reigning. Worship leaders were getting pregnant. Altar workers were addicted to crack cocaine and stealing money from the church. Others in leadership had been arrested for fake license plates and expired driver's licenses. Others were in government investigations for massive fraud. One guy was even caught on film in an armed robbery.

Well, when I started talking about the problems, I became the problem. When I suggested that Jezebel had a toehold in the church, I was attacked. I was later cursed publicly and told that I would never succeed if I left that church. I was told I would lose my anointing. I was told I flowed in a Jezebel spirit. That was the spirit of Jezebel trying to intimidate me, discredit me, and silence my voice. I was exposing Jezebel's operations and that spirit worked to shut me down. But I overcame.

How can I recognize the influence of the spirit of Jezebel in a church?

In a church setting, you'll see Jezebel's influence in a couple of ways. Where sexual sin is abounding, Jezebel is often pulling the strings. Jezebel also sets up pastors as idols, rock stars who can't be questioned, while working behind the scenes to cause that pastor to fall so that the saints will be disillusioned. You can see this in stories about megachurch pastors caught up in immorality or Ponzi schemes or other sins.

How can we head off the spirit of Jezebel? For example, if we discern someone has come into the prayer group and has a Jezebelic influence on their life, what can we do before it causes damage?

The best thing to do is shut it down in prayer. We have authority in the spirit in the territory God has given us. If you are the head intercessor or a faithful intercessor in a group and discern something, you can go into prayer.

I would pray:

> *Lord, if this person is not willing to repent of Jezebelic influences, if You didn't send them here for the sake of deliverance, if they are on assignment from the enemy to disrupt, I forbid them from any and all attempts to move against Your will. Let their tongue cleave to the roof of*

their mouth before they speak words or pray prayers against Your will. Lord, encounter this person's heart with Your love and heal their wounds.

In the natural, you can also have a guardian over the prayer mic who decides who prays and who doesn't pray. You don't have to have an open mic or open prayer. You can choose to call on those who can pray. This is part of knowing those who labor among you (see 1 Thess. 5:12).

Remember, many people who are operating under Jezebelic influences do not know. They are blind to their own deception. They may sincerely believe they are praying for the will of God, yet when they pray they are like a bull in a china shop doing damage. There's a difference in how you deal with someone who is intentionally working to bring harm and someone who is blinded to their infirmity.

This is part of what makes it so dangerous. We don't want to hurt and wound someone more. It can be a fine line and we need to be Spirit-led and walk in love and kindness. Remember, it's the kindness of God that leads people to repentance (see Rom. 2:4).

How do you get someone delivered from a Jezebel spirit?

You need to get someone healed from the hurts and wounds that allowed this spirit to gain a stronghold in their mind. You can check out my book *Deliverance from the Jezebel Spirit* to learn more about this timely topic.

Was the Jezebel in the Book of Revelation a Christian?

We don't really know. Jezebel may have been a Christian who had the same spirit that was influencing Queen Jezebel centuries earlier. Or she may have been an unbeliever who infiltrated the ranks of the church. Either way, Jesus gave her a space to repent.

ABOUT
JENNIFER LECLAIRE

Jennifer LeClaire is senior leader of Awakening House of Prayer in Fort Lauderdale, Florida, founder of the Ignite Network, and founder of the Awakening Prayer Hubs prayer movement. Jennifer formerly served as the first-ever female editor of *Charisma* magazine and is a prolific author of over 50 books. You can find Jennifer online or shoot her an email at info@jenniferleclaire.org.

YOUR Prophetic COMMUNITY

Sign up for **FREE** Subscription to the Destiny Image digital magazine, and get awesome content delivered directly to your inbox!

destinyimage.com/signup

Sign-up for Cutting-Edge Messages that Supernaturally Empower You

- Gain valuable insights and guidance based on biblical principles
- Deepen your faith and understanding of God's plan for your life
- Receive regular updates and prophetic messages
- Connect with a community of believers who share your values and beliefs

Experience Fresh Video Content that Strengthens Your Prophetic Inheritance

- Receive prophetic messages and insights
- Connect with a powerful tool for spiritual growth and development
- Stay connected and inspired on your faith journey

Listen to Powerful Podcasts that Equips You for God's Presence Everyday

- Deepen your understanding of God's prophetic assignment
- Experience God's revival power throughout your day
- Learn how to grow spiritually in your walk with God

Check out our **Destiny Image** bestsellers page at
destinyimage.com/bestsellers

for cutting-edge, prophetic messages that will supernaturally empower you and the body of Christ.

In the Right Hands, This Book Will Change Lives!

Most of the people who need this message will not be looking for this book. To change their lives, you need to **put a copy of this book in their hands.**

Our ministry is constantly seeking methods to find the people who need this anointed message to change their lives. **Will you help us reach these people?**

Extend this ministry by sowing 3 books, 5 books, 10 books, or more today, and become a life changer! Your generosity will be part of catalyzing the Great Awakening that many have been prophesying and praying for.

Manufactured by Amazon.ca
Bolton, ON